Endorsements

Rhonda (Mrs. Danny) Sinquefield—Minister's wife for thirty-one years. She is the pastor's wife at Faith Baptist Church, Bartlett, Tennessee (Joyce's pastor's wife). She has taught fifth-grade Sunday School and Bible Drill for over twenty-five years.

> This book is not only informational, but inspirational and practical. Every minister's wife will benefit from the encouragement to discover and develop their uniqueness and also to realize the importance of studying and knowing God's Word.

Susie (Mrs. O. S.) Hawkins—Pastor's wife for twenty-two years, forty as a ministry wife. Presently her husband is the president of Guidestone in Dallas, Texas. She is an advocate for ministry wives, is a speaker and author, and began the Widows' Might Ministry, enlisting widows of ministers to pray for Southern Baptists around the world.

> This book is full of humor, practical wisdom, and great spiritual insight. The journey Joyce and Adrian shared through years of ministry is a story of incredible love and commitment between a husband, a wife, and their Lord. I eagerly encourage all ministry wives to read this much-needed book!

Jodie (Mrs. Morris) Chapman—Pastor's wife for twenty-seven years. For eighteen years her husband served as the President of the Executive Committee of the Southern Baptist Convention (SBC). Jodie served on the Peace Committee of the SBC, 1985–1987.

Joyce has written great nuggets of God's truths for all wives of ministers and also for any wife in any position, whether in or out of the ministry. I wish I had had this book when Morris and I were serving in our first church. Thanks, Joyce. "Iron sharpens iron…" (Proverbs 27:17).

Janet (Mrs. Hayes) Wicker—Pastor's wife for thirty-seven years. Janet is married to the senior pastor of First Baptist Church of Naples, Florida. She teaches weekly Bible studies to the women of her church through a ministry call RefresHer and is an author. Janet served as the president of the SBC Ministers' Wives Fellowship in 2012.

Joyce has written a wonderful resource for pastors' wives that is practically useful, beautifully transparent, and personally intimate. Her words touched my heart with moments of laughter along with times of quiet tears. Most precious to me is the chapter entitled, "Lessons I Learned from Adrian," reminding us all that our husbands are also our pastors whose sermons, teachings, and very lives testify to us of God's great glory!

Carol Ann (Mrs. Jimmy) Draper—Pastor's wife for thirty-five years, fifty-six years in ministry. Her husband served for fifteen years as the president of LifeWay Resources. She is a gifted speaker, teacher, and encourager of wives, especially those in ministry.

I experienced all the things that Joyce addresses in this excellent guide for pastors' wives. In all the challenges, disappointments, struggles, and wonderful blessings, this book will encourage and inspire every pastor's wife for her journey in ministry with her preacher husband.

To Kelsie,
Love in Jesus
Joyce Rogers
Ps. 18:29

Chosen to Be a Minister's Wife

Joyce Rogers

innovo PUBLISHING

Published by
Innovo Publishing, LLC
www.innovopublishing.com
1-888-546-2111

Providing Full-Service Publishing Services for
Christian Authors, Artists & Organizations: Hardbacks, Paperbacks,
eBooks, Audiobooks, Music & Videos

CHOSEN TO BE A MINISTER'S WIFE

Library of Congress Control Number: 2013932045
ISBN 13: 978-1-61314-067-3

Cover Design & Interior Layout: Innovo Publishing, LLC

Printed in the United States of America
U.S. Printing History

First Edition: February 2013

Dedication

To that wonderful man, Adrian, my husband and pastor for fifty-four years. I pay tribute to him, from whom I learned life-changing lessons too numerous to count.

He was a lover of God's Word—the living Word of God, the LORD Jesus, and the written Word of God—the Bible. He was a JESUS man. Largely because of him, I am a JESUS woman and a lover of Him and His written Word.

Ultimately, this book is dedicated to the God-man, whom we both loved and served together—JESUS!

To the multitude of ministers' wives who serve alongside their husbands, "standing in the shadows."

To three lifetime friends—faithful and loving pastor's wives: Joyce (Mrs. Joe) Boatwright, Johnnie (Mrs. Peter) Lord, and Barbara (Mrs. Bob) Barwick. "I will always love you and your dear husbands!"

To two wonderful pastor's wives who walked faithfully beside their husbands in our youth and were such role models for me: Elsie Jean (Mrs. Guy) Marlowe and Betty (Mrs. Alan) Watson.

To my special friend, Dot (Mrs. Tom) Clayton who, along with her husband, labored with us for many years on staff at First Baptist Church in Merritt Island, Florida, and then at Bellevue Baptist Church in Memphis, Tennessee. She was one of my greatest encouragers. She is in heaven now along with her precious Tom, fellowshipping with Adrian.

Appreciation

I would like to express my heartfelt appreciation to:

Innovo Publishing: Bart Dahmer for believing in my project; Darya Crockett for her tremendous patience and help in editing my manuscript; and Terry Bailey for her encouragement, support, and expertise throughout this project.

The pastors' wives who read my manuscript and gave such supportive endorsements: My pastor's wife, Rhonda (Mrs. Danny) Sinquefied; Jodie (Mrs. Morris) Chapman; Carol Ann (Mrs. Jimmy) Draper; Susie (Mrs. O. S.) Hawkins; and Janet (Mrs. Hayes) Wicker.

My longtime friend, Ruth Ann Shelton, who introduced me to Innovo Publishing and has been such an encouragement to me.

My children and other family members who have loved me and allowed me to use them as illustrations.

My sister, Doris, who is my greatest prayer partner and wonderful example of trusting Jesus for her every need.

My gifted young friend, Melanie Redd, who first read my manuscript and encouraged me to have it published.

My special friend in ministry, Sarah Maddox, who has stood beside me in reaching out to ministers' wives and many other women.

Thanks so much!

Much love, Joyce

Preface

This book originally began when I taught these truths to a group of ministers' wives who attended the Adrian Rogers Pastor Training Institute with their husbands in the years 2003–2005. I adapted and expanded my teaching notes into book form.

I have had a special desire to reach out to the younger generation of pastors' wives and other ministry wives to share with them the many lessons I have learned in fifty-four years of ministry as a pastor's wife.

It is my desire that many wives will be encouraged and blessed by the message in this book.

Table of Contents

The Challenge of Being the Minister's Wife

Living with a minister has been described as "living in a fishbowl." Some don't want or like the scrutiny that comes with this role. Some resist the pressure and dare to live however they wish. I even heard of one pastor's wife who played tennis during church. She obviously disregarded her example.

Giving up one's so-called rights and joyfully giving oneself to this calling will be pleasing to Jesus and can also be very rewarding. Others *are* observing the way you dress. No, you don't have to be unstylish, but dressing modestly will be a powerful example to other women and their daughters. *Appropriate* is a good word to use as a guideline. One's clothes should not be too tight or too bare, skirts and dresses too short, or necklines too low (showing your cleavage), which accentuates your female anatomy. Dress to please and honor your husband. Ask him what he thinks is appropriate if you are in doubt. Don't assume that the current styles are all right for a Christian to wear. Above all, dress and act to please your Savior. Colossians 3:17 is an outstanding guideline. *"And whatsoever ye do in word or deed, do all in the name of the Lord Jesus, giving thanks to God and the Father by Him."* Dress and act in such a way that people won't be surprised when they discover that you are the minister's wife. Consider your position a privilege—a special place that God has given you to be an example for Him!

CHAPTER 1

The Lord Shall Choose for Me

I was a pastor's wife for fifty-four years, and I loved this calling. That does not mean that I have had no problems or frustrations, but God has been faithful and has taught me many lessons. I would like to share some of my testimony about the path on which God has brought me, including two of the greatest lessons I have learned along the way.

Early Years

I met Adrian Rogers in the fourth grade, but it was not until the sixth grade that I took note of him. It was then that he began to drop love notes by my desk. That must have impressed me because I still have those notes, and I am *Mrs.* Adrian Rogers.

When Adrian was sixteen years old and I was fifteen, our pastor and his wife took us to Ridgecrest, North Carolina, to our Baptist Assembly.

I was standing by Adrian's side the evening he stepped out to declare that he felt God was calling him to preach the gospel. There was no one in the world any happier than I.

The next day my pastor asked me why I had not gone forward also. He said, "You know that a preacher's wife must be called too." We were too young to make that kind of a declaration, but I went with Adrian to the follow-up meeting that afternoon. I signed a card saying I felt called into full-time Christian service because I really did. I checked the box that said "undecided" about which field of Christian service, but deep in my heart I knew that one day I would be Mrs. Adrian Rogers, pastor's wife.

Joyce, engaged at seventeen years old

College, Marriage, and Our First Church—First Baptist Church of Fellsmere, Florida

Adrian was called to our first church toward the end of our first year in college—First Baptist Church of Fellsmere, Florida. We were married at the beginning of our second year of college.

I became a pastor's wife when I was just eighteen years old. I loved being a pastor's wife, and I loved being his wife. I taught all of the teenagers and planned recreation every Saturday night in the churchyard for all of the young people in town. There were only about five hundred people in that little town.

I will never forget the church and those people. We spent each weekend in the homes of some of the members. We went back some years ago for their fiftieth anniversary. The pastor who was there had been a ten-year-old boy when we were first there. I even have old movies of him at that age. That experience was wonderful!

College and Our First Baby—Steve

I went to two more years of college and completed all of the subjects in my major, which was religion. We then decided we wanted to have a baby. I reasoned that I would go to the seminary for a year instead of finishing college.

Adrian graduated from college with his BA. I was seated in the audience holding my BA–BY, my BABY that is. Stephen Michael Rogers was then three months old. We were so blessed.

Seminary—Two More Babies, Gayle and Philip

Adrian then enrolled in the New Orleans Baptist Seminary. Waiting for seminary housing to open, we stayed two weeks with friends, Bob and Barbara Barwick, sleeping on their box springs while they slept on the top mattress. Then we moved into the Florida Avenue Housing Project, along with one hundred other seminary families. We were grateful to move in even though we discovered a few disadvantages.

Joyce and Adrian cutting their wedding cake

Steve was still in diapers. There were no disposable diapers back then. I hung them on the line. But we were warned to not leave any laundry on the clothesline at night lest it be stolen.

After six months, Adrian was called to the Waveland Baptist Chapel in Waveland, Mississippi, which was sixty miles from the seminary. We moved onto the "church field" and Adrian commuted to school Tuesday through Friday, while I stayed home.

The Waveland Chapel had twenty-five members when we arrived, but around one hundred when we left three and a half years later when Adrian graduated from seminary. We learned to love these people, and I will never forget those years.

Steve at seven months old;
Joyce hanging diapers

We didn't even realize in those days that we were poor. Sometimes I was lonely, but I met a doctor's wife with small children who lived nearby, and we became friends. Then we met the pastor and his wife from our sponsoring church in Bay St. Louis. We became good friends and got together every weekend we could.

However, I never made it to the seminary like I had planned. Instead, we had two more babies, Gayle Christine, followed by Philip Gentry. I have always been a student though, and I studied on my own. I would listen to the *Back to the Bible* radio broadcast, featuring Theodore Epp. I ordered their correspondence courses. God greatly used these lessons in my life, and I received great instruction in the Bible.

Park View Baptist Church

Adrian then graduated from seminary and we accepted a call to Park View Baptist Church in Fort Pierce, Florida. They had one hundred in Sunday School and a little parsonage right next to the church. I thought it was wonderful.

Philip's Death

It was Mother's Day, and we had been at our new church for just three weeks. Steve was now four years old, Gayle was two, and little Philip was just two and a half months old. I had finished washing the dishes. The children were asleep, and I was getting ready to take a nap. I glanced in the baby's crib, and he looked so strange. I called for Adrian to come quickly. Horrified, I asked, "Is he dead?"

Adrian said, "You stay here," because the other children were asleep. He tucked little Philip inside his coat and drove as fast as he could to the hospital.

I was there "alone with God." Immediately, a Bible verse came to my mind. It was Job 1:21: *"The LORD gave, and the LORD has taken away; blessed be the name of the LORD."* Then the twenty-third Psalm, which I had memorized as a child, rushed to my rescue. I came to verse four, *"Yea, though I walk through the valley of the shadow of death, I will fear no evil; For You are with me; Your rod and Your staff, they comfort me."* I understood for the first time in my life what that really meant. Yes, He was there with me. I felt His presence.

In a very short time, I saw Adrian coming up the front sidewalk, and I knew by the look on his face that our little Philip was gone—gone to be with Jesus. We had this inscription put on his grave marker: "Philip! Yes, Lord!" God called him and he answered, "Yes!"

Gayle, Adrian, Philip, Steve, and Joyce

First Lesson in My Life—How to Give Up My Right to Understand Why

It was in the days to follow that I learned the first great lesson in my life—how to give up my right to understand why. Three factors helped me in this step of faith. I *leaned hard on Jesus*, the Living Word of God. I cried out to Him. I needed Him like I had never needed Him before, and He was there! In this experience, I learned how to *praise God by faith* when I did not *feel* like

17

it. During those days, the book of Psalms became my favorite book in the Bible. God especially spoke to me through Psalm 63:3–4 which says, *"Because Your lovingkindness is better than life, My lips shall praise You. Thus will I bless You while I live; I will lift up my hands in Your name."*

The second factor that helped me was *God's wonderful written Word, the Bible.* I had faithfully read my Bible since I was a child, but I now dug deep into this marvelous treasure Book. It contained help and hope for my broken heart. Oh, how I love His Word.

The third factor that helped bring me comfort was *music.* I love music. I searched the hymnal and other songbooks for songs that would minister to my need. I would sit at the piano, play simple songs, and sing them to the Lord. They helped me verbalize my prayers and my praise. There were many songs God used in my life. But there was one song in particular that helped me give up my so-called right to understand why. It was titled, "We'll Talk It Over" by Ira Stanphill. He had suffered a great heartbreak in his own life. This song was his testimony, and it greatly touched my heart and life.

WE'LL TALK IT OVER [1]

Tho' shadows deepen and my heart bleeds
I will not question the way He leads.
This side of heaven we know in part
I will not question a broken heart.

We'll talk it over in the bye and bye
We'll talk it over, my Lord and I;
I'll ask the reasons
He'll tell me why
When we talk it over
In the bye and bye.

---

[1] Words and music by Ira Stanphill, 1949.

I experienced great victory in the midst of great grief. As both Adrian and I cast ourselves completely on Jesus day by day, He taught us many precious truths about Himself and the Spirit-filled life.

In exchange for giving up my right to understand why, I believe God gave me a song of comfort and joy for myself and also to sing for others. The words and the melody may change, but that inner song has never left my life.

God began to bring about a spiritual deepening in our lives, and in our church we began to focus on Jesus and depend on Him in a way we had never done before. This truly was a watershed experience in our lives and ministry. We would never be the same.

Birth of David and Janice

Two years passed, and God gave us another baby boy. We named him David, which means, "beloved." He became a missionary to Spain for eighteen years.

His sister, Janice, was born sixteen months later. I almost miscarried both of them, and I spent two months during each pregnancy in bed for the first few months. I could not do anything during those days. I had to get full-time help for a while.

God brought many life-changing books into my life in those days. The great lesson that I learned in those days was that it was more important to *be* than to *do*. One very significant book that I read in those days was *The Calvary Road* by Roy Hession. It was about the self-life and how to recognize these sins and bring them to the cross.

A young Janice and David

19

More Victory

In spite of my grief, God gave me great victory, and I loved being a minister's wife. Adrian and I had done everything together—led the young people, gone visiting together, etc. But when the fourth baby came, and so close behind the third, I had to give up my youth work, and almost everything, for a while.

Move to First Baptist Church of Merritt Island, Florida

Our church in Fort Pierce had grown from one hundred to six hundred in six years. When we accepted the call to First Baptist Church of Merritt Island, it had fewer in attendance, but it had a great potential for growth. We served there during the Apollo Series, when man went to the moon. In fact, we stood in our backyard and watched the moon launch. Those were exciting days!

Several times in those early years, I had said that I never wanted to go to a big church, but gradually this church grew into a big church.

The Rogers' four young children in Merritt Island, FL

I was busy with the children. I had begun to teach again—young married women. But we hardly did anything in ministry together anymore. The more the church grew, the busier Adrian became. He was gone almost every evening.

And guess what? I began to feel left out and unneeded. I tried to tell him this, but he didn't understand. He told me he did need me—at home.

He began to add staff members. With every new staff member he would tell me things like, "We have a music director now; don't ask to sing." "We have an educational director now; don't share your ideas about Sunday school," etc.

On and on it went, until I became very frustrated because I loved every aspect of the church. I at least wanted to be informed and able to share my ideas with my husband. I didn't want to be on the staff. I just wanted to feel needed in this part of his life.

I finally went to talk to Johnnie Lord, a good friend who was also a pastor's wife, who lived in the next town. She recommended that I call a Christian counselor, who was in the area for the week with Campus Crusade for Christ. He came to our house one evening and talked to us for several hours. He ended by saying to me, "Mrs. Rogers, you are a very bitter woman." I started to reply, "No, I'm very frustrated," but God put His finger on my heart and said inwardly, "He's right!"

It was then I realized that although I loved my role as a pastor's wife, I did not love being in this church that had grown into a big church, where my husband was so busy that I felt left out.

Second Lesson—How to Give Up My Right to be Understood

That was only the beginning of my victory. Complete victory finally came some months later at a women's retreat when a minister's wife "prayed me through" to victory, and I gave up my so-called right to be understood. I realized God had given me a wonderful gift in exchange—the gift of understanding ministers' wives, and even wives of busy executives and doctors, whose husbands were gone a lot.

By and by, God gave Adrian a lot of understanding regarding my needs, for which I was grateful. And I, too, gained a great deal of understanding of his needs. But God could not excuse my bitterness. I will always be grateful for Dr. Henry Brandt, who told it like it was. I thanked him many times through the years. He is in heaven now. One day I will see him there, and when I do, I will thank him again.

Call to Bellevue Baptist Church, Memphis, Tennessee

About a year later a telephone call came about going to a big, historic church—Bellevue Baptist Church—that had in its past a world famous preacher, Dr. Robert G. Lee. In fact, when we were in high school we had gone to hear him preach when he came to town.

The first words out of my mouth were, "Oh, no!" But it was as if God put His hand on my shoulder and said much louder than words, "Don't be a fool after all I have taught you in this past year." So immediately I said, "Yes, Lord!" I knew in my heart, even before Adrian, that this was God's will for our lives. I am sure it was because I yielded to God that I was so happy in what later grew into what I lovingly called a "monster church."

I still remember when we first came to Bellevue, walking down the halls with many older ladies patting me on the shoulder and telling me they loved me. I asked Adrian, "How can they love me when they don't even know me?" I concluded that they loved me by faith and I loved them back. That resulted in a thirty-two-year love affair with those wonderful people.

I did not have the background to make me always feel comfortable with the demands that came to my life during the ensuing years, but God stretched me and grew me to make me adequate. *"You have relieved me in my distress; Have mercy on me, and hear my prayer"* (Psalm 4:1b). I discovered who I was as a person and how God wanted to use me in my own unique way.

When we first went to Bellevue, two previous retired pastors were still members of the church, Dr. Robert G. Lee and Dr. Ramsey Pollard and his wife, Della. I remember visiting in the home of the Pollards and being shown around. I noticed many serving pieces of silver and china and was told what a gracious entertainer she was. I whispered in Adrian's ear, "I can't be like this." And he whispered back, "And I don't want you to be." What a freeing moment that was!

As the years came and went, I was given many beautiful pieces of silver and china. When Mrs. Pollard died, Dr. Pollard gave me a beautiful china tea set that matched my own china pattern. God helped me to reach out and ask others to help me, and I was eventually able to feel comfortable entertaining in our home. But my predominate gifts lay elsewhere, and God used me in other areas that fit into who I was in Christ.

I could never have dreamed what opportunities, challenges, and tremendous victories would come to our lives as we served in this church. All I can say is, "Thank you, Jesus, for all You have done. I give You all the glory."

The Lord Shall Choose for Me

No, I would have not chosen to go to a big church, but God had other plans. I was called upon to submit to Him and ask Him to lead and guide me on His path, not mine. I love this song that expresses this so well.

SUBMISSION [2]

The path that I have trod
Has brought me nearer God
Tho' oft it led through sorrow's gates.
Tho' not the way I'd choose
In my way I might lose
The joy that yet for me awaits.

---

[2] The Rodeheaver Co., copyright renewal 1962. Used by permission.

Not what I wish to be
Nor where I wish to go;
For who am I that I
Should choose my way?
The Lord shall choose for me
'Tis better far I know;
Then let Him bid me go or stay.

—C. Austin Miles

Joyce and Adrian's 32nd anniversary at Bellevue

CHAPTER 2

The Greatest Resource for the Minister's Wife

Is it just the pastor who should have knowledge of the Word of God? Although not to the same degree, the pastor's wife needs to also know and love the Bible. As she saturates her life with the promises and truths from its pages, she will bear witness that God's Word is true.

For Her Own Life

This is imperative for her own life. Time spent each day searching God's wonderful treasure Book and asking Him to speak to her personally is vital. In this way, she can have an intimate relationship with God. Secondhand knowledge of Him—depending on her husband's experience and knowledge of the Word—is not sufficient.

From His Word

When experiences shake your life and your faith, you need to be convinced for yourself that God's promises are true. When my baby died many years ago, it was Job 1:21 from God's Word that first came to my mind. *"The LORD gave, and the LORD has taken away; Blessed be the name of the LORD."* This was an encouragement to me to praise the LORD in the midst of my deep grief. Then Psalm 23 rushed to my rescue from the inner recesses of my mind and spirit. I had memorized it as a child. I remember crying it out loud to Jesus, my good Shepherd.

I then dug deeper into God's Word. My broken heart cried out to go deeper and to know Him better. From His written Word, I learned how to praise Him even when I didn't feel like it. I "faithed" my praise to God, and one day I realized that I felt like praising Him.

As I searched His treasure Book, He spoke to my heart over and over again. He taught me from His extraordinary truth. He showed me that His loving-kindness was better than life itself (Psalm 63:3). When my beloved husband of fifty-four years took his heavenly flight, I claimed this wonderful promise again—in my present circumstance, the darkest hour of my life. You could never convince me that it is not true because I have experienced God's loving-kindness for myself.

He convinced me that there was a multitude of His mercies (Psalm 51:1; Lamentations 3:32) and that they were new every morning (Lamentations 3:23).

When God called home the one whom I had loved since I was a child, He reminded me from His Word that He would never leave me nor forsake me (Hebrews 13:5). His name, JEHOVAH SHAMMAH, assured me that it was so! It means, "The LORD is there." His Word whispered to my heart, "It is true! It is true." I have claimed this promise over and over again, and I now know from experience that indeed, "It is true!"

His Word taught me what God is like. He is good. He is merciful and compassionate. He is righteous and holy. I learned from His Word that God was my Savior and my strength, my help and my hope, my refuge and my high tower.

Because I learned about Who He was and what He was like, I came to trust Him, even when I didn't understand why. The life of Job was such an example to me. I believe that the greatest declaration of faith in the Bible was made by Job when he said, *"Though He slay me, yet will I trust Him"* (Job 13:15).

Years ago, someone challenged me to search to know what God is like from the book of Psalms. I bought a notebook to record what I found.

I read a Psalm each day and wrote down only the character traits of God. Then I praised Him for what I discovered. What a blessing that was to me! I encourage you to do the same.

I have read Bill Bright's wonderful book, *God: Discover His Character*, twice. He writes about thirteen character qualities of God. I was so blessed as I studied and contemplated each quality and gave thanks to my magnificent God for Who He is and what He is like. I encourage you to study this wonderful book.

From His Word, I learned how to pray and to praise Him; to give thanks for everything He has given to me; and to confess my sins on a daily basis so I can remain clean before God. I realized the importance of praying for others and of the necessity to forgive those who have wronged me, even when what they did broke my heart.

I studied the types of Christ and how characters in the Bible portrayed the character of my Savior. I learned to walk with Him in my daily life as He revealed Himself to me through His written Word.

God taught me from His Word that in His presence is fullness of joy—that joy isn't found in possessions or people but only in Him. Only when some who were dearest to me were taken away did this prove to be so!

From His Word, He revealed to me that I was a part of the bride of Christ. But He also showed me that He had a special spiritual relationship with the widow. He had a special name shown to her—JEHOVAH SABAOTH—which means *"The LORD of Hosts"* (Isaiah 54:5). In that name, I am assured of His protection and His power—assured that He will fight my battles for me. I had shared this truth with many widows before Adrian died. One day, soon after Adrian was gone, I decided to share it with myself. I claimed this promise as my very own.

Indeed, I took Jesus to be my spiritual Husband. Many a time, I have asked Him to put His spiritual arms around me and to embrace me with His love. And do you know, He does!

I always felt that I was safe with Adrian. He was courageous, and he was strong. I knew that he would be there for me. But when God called him home, I had this inward assurance that God would never leave me.

I remember telling Adrian toward the end, "I'll be all right." I don't believe he heard me, and I didn't know exactly what all that statement involved. But deep in my heart I knew God would be there for me, and He has! Hasn't He promised this in His Word? This truth has been hidden in my heart for years, and no one can ever steal it away from me.

I was taught from His Word that the greatest of all the commandments is to love God with all my heart, mind, and soul. I learned that God is love and that the way to dwell in God is to dwell in love.

It is from His Word that I know He first loved me (1 John 4:19). One of the very first Bible verses I memorized as a child was John 3:16: *"For God so loved the world that He gave His only begotten Son, that whoever believes in Him should not perish but have everlasting life."*

Because of His great love, I gave all there was of Joyce to all there was of Jesus when I was just a little nine-year-old girl. I've never regretted that day when I surrendered my life to Him. He has never disappointed me! He is still my first and greatest Love.

From His Word I learned that the second greatest commandment was to love others and to share the gospel with them—the good news that Jesus died for their sins, that He was buried and rose again from the dead. I long for my loved ones and friends to know the gospel, to yield their lives to the Lover of their souls and to love Him with all their hearts, souls, and minds.

We try to get the cart before the horse. We try to love others before we love God. It is impossible. I learned it from the Bible. Try God's plan. It works!

Oh, I've learned so many other things for my life from God's Word. I've learned that when I am in trouble I can run to Him and hide (Psalm 61:2–3); that when my heart is tossed and troubled, Jesus is my peace (Ephesians 2:14); and that when I am lonely He is there (Isaiah 43:2).

Everything I need to know I find in Him. His written Word tells me all about Him. Yes, the pastor's wife needs to know, believe, obey, and memorize God's precious Word for all the trials that will come her way.

That Others May Know

The minister's wife also needs to know God's Word so that she can share with others and minister to them. The congregation is looking not only to the pastor but also to his wife to see her example—how she handles life's trials and traumas. Does what the pastor preaches from the pulpit work in how his wife handles the vicissitudes and storms of life?

Yes, we live in a fishbowl; others are watching us. But don't focus on that fact. They just want to know if what you profess is real. If it is, your life will encourage them to trust God when the storms of life shake them to the core.

A few years ago a young woman, whom I didn't even know, came up to me at church. She wanted to thank me for my example. I had no idea that she was watching or what she saw. I have learned over the years not to focus on others and what they think. I need only to have a longing to please Jesus and leave the rest to Him.

The Rogers family—Adrian and Joyce's 50th wedding anniversary

Your Children

Those who are closest to you want to know if what you teach is true. Yes, you need to teach your children to study and learn God's Word. But most of all, are they learning from you that God's promises are true—that Mom can not only recite them but also claim them and live them out in her daily life?

Do they hear you witness to the waitress or the repairman? Do they see you prepare and take a meal to someone who is sick or who had a loved one die? Do they hear you pray for those who are sick, unsaved, or in trouble?

Years ago, I wrote out verses in a little 3 x 5 spiral book for my daughter, Janice. She was expecting her first baby, and I had found verses about deliverance. Years later, I made one for each of her two oldest daughters, Angie and Rachel, when they were going through times of trouble. Now, Janice makes Scripture rings[3] (about thirty verses) to give to those going through trouble. Sometimes I go over to her house and help put these Scripture verses together. One day, her eight-year-old daughter, Breanna, had made her own Bible verse on colorful paper. She had printed on it: *"The joy of the LORD is your strength"* (Nehemiah 8:10). She gave it to me. I use it as a bookmark in my Bible. It is one of my greatest treasures! Some years later, Rachel created her own colorful, handmade book, listing promises from God's Word. This is how we can lead by example.

I love the names for God—both Old and New. If you visited Janice's home, you would see a number of these names placed around her home. Rachel designs favorite names for God and favorite Bible verses or slogans for the home.

Do your children know you love and believe God's Word? Do they know you claim its promises for their lives?

Your Friends and Acquaintances

Do you just chat with your friends and acquaintances—perhaps go shopping or participate in your favorite hobby with them? Or do you sometimes share your deep love of God's Word with them? Do they know you are a woman of the Word? Do they know you live by the Word of God?

I have written numerous notes during our years of ministry to the sick and sorrowful, to those who are celebrating weddings and the birth of a baby. They were filled with words of blessing and encouragement from God's Word.

Sometimes I will read a verse out of God's Word over the phone to someone in need. I've even sung God's promises to others over the phone or at the hospital bedside.

---

[3] Scripture rings are typewritten verses, hole-punched and put on a metal ring.

Your Pastor Husband

I could always ask my pastor/husband any question about the Bible or ask him where any passage was. He always knew the answers to my questions. I guess he was my own personal built-in Bible commentary and concordance. But I also encouraged him with promises from God's Word. He kept them near.

I have always held on to the promises in God's Word. I knew that God would never leave me nor forsake me because His Word told me so, and I believed that promise (Hebrews 13:5).

Do not compare your husband to other pastors. Be aware of the special qualities that make your pastor/husband unique and express your gratitude to him for these.

- Is he a compassionate man?
- Does he have a special gift of faith?
- Does he love children and make efforts to include them in his personal contact and preaching?
- Is he a man of deep conviction and courage?
- Does he tend to details?
- Is he a man of humility and integrity?

I lived for fifty-four years with a man who loved, lived, believed, and preached God's Word. After Adrian went home to be with the Lord, I ran as fast as I could into the arms of Jesus, the Living Word of God, and I dug deeper into the treasure chest of His written Word. Yes, Jesus is enough!

I Know God's Word is True!

I know God's Word is true! In life's valleys, I have clung to His promises, and Jesus has always been there.

Some of the promises I have returned to over and over again are:

"Yea, though I walk through the valley of the shadow of death, I will fear no evil, For You are with me" (Psalm 23:4).

"Because Your lovingkindness is better than life, my lips shall praise You" (Psalm 63:3).

"For by You I can run against a troop, by my God I can leap over a wall" (Psalm 18:29).

"Happy is he (she) who has the God of Jacob for his (her) help, whose hope is in the LORD *his (her) God"* (Psalm 146:5).

"When you pass through the waters, I will be with you; and through the rivers, they shall not overflow you. When you walk through the fire, you shall not be burned, nor shall the flame scorch you. Fear not: for I am with you . . . " (Isaiah 43:2, 5).

"The LORD *is my strength and my shield; my heart trusted in Him, and I am helped; therefore my heart greatly rejoices, and with my song will I praise Him"* (Psalm 28:7).

I have hidden God's Word in my heart since I was a child. But I have continued to study, believe, and memorize it. It has run to my rescue too many times to count. The Word of God is my greatest help. I can only say along with the psalmist, *"I love Your law"* (Psalm 119:113b).

CHAPTER 3

Discovering and Developing Your Uniqueness

"A successful minister's wife is one who not only tactfully and wholeheartedly supports her husband in his ministry without usurping in any way his function, but one who also complements him by daring to stir up the gifts that are in her."—Helen Shoemaker

I'm told there was a pastor's wife who had an identity problem and an energy crisis at the same time. She didn't know who she was, and she was too tired to find out.

We're going to try to answer two questions. Who am I? and What is my role?

Who Am I?

A Unique Person

My children call me *Mom*.
My husband called me *Sweetheart or Honey*.
My sister calls me *Sis*.
My friends call me *Joyce*.

Some church members called me *Mrs. Rogers.*
Others referred to me as *the pastor's wife.*
Some lovingly called me *Mrs. Preacher.*

Indeed, I am a combination of all of these and more. There are many unspoken expectations of who I ought to be.

- My husband's expectations
- My children's expectations
- The church member's expectations
- My own expectations
- God's expectations

When I was a young pastor's wife, all of these expectations brought conflict, and my heart cried out, "I've got to be me. I've just got to be me!" Then I adjusted that cry to, "I've got to be me—in Christ—who He made me to be!"

I also discovered that I was a complicated me, and on top of it all, some of the factors in my life were constantly changing.

But I am unique! You are unique—one of a kind.

What Is My Role?

I was a pastor's wife for fifty-four years. I loved my role. But I discovered many years ago that there is no copy or mold for the minister's wife. We come in all sizes and shapes. We have different talents, temperaments, and spiritual gifts. We come from different backgrounds and have different training. Some are dynamic Bible teachers, some are gracious entertainers, others are great nursery and children's workers, and some are wonderful listeners and counselors.

We are also a combination of:

- Our personality or temperament type
- Our inborn talents
- Our spiritual gifts and spiritual experiences
- Our family background
- Our education and training
- Our life experiences

Psalm 139:14 says, *"I will praise You, for I am fearfully and wonderfully made."* We are each a "Designer creation." We have a special label—Made by God.

Four Temperament Types

There are four temperament types that are commonly accepted.

Choleric—strong, leadership type
Sanguine—outgoing, friendly type
Phlegmatic—easygoing type
Melancholy—sensitive, creative type

No one is just one type. We are a unique combination of these, but we probably have a predominant temperament type. There are strengths and weaknesses with each type. If you haven't read Tim and Beverly LaHaye's books on the temperaments, you ought to read them. They emphasize that there is strength for every weakness by being filled with the Holy Spirit.

Innate Talents

The ministers' wives that I know have many and varied talents. I recently met a pastor's wife who had an extraordinary ability to paint. Someone else I know is a gifted pianist; another has a beautiful voice. One of my best friends has the gift of counseling and prayer. Some have the gift of organization, teaching, or writing. Some work with children; some, with young people; others, with adults. No, not every minister's wife can play the piano, but you name it, and some minister's wife has that talent.

You may have discovered your major talents when you were young—but not necessarily. Sometimes we don't discover all of our talents until we get older. Remember Grandma Moses who started painting when she was in her seventies? She captured the hearts of the heartland people with her scenes of folk art.

I am about to turn eighty years old as I work on this book. In my mind, I think I'm fifty-five. Praise the Lord! You can use your talents as you move through the different seasons of your life. Never say you are through. God is never finished with you here until He takes you on to heaven.

Spiritual Gifts and Spiritual Life

Spiritual gifts were not being taught in Baptist churches when I was younger. There are many resources on this subject today. Some years ago, I identified my predominant spiritual gifts—exhortation and mercy. Discovering what my spiritual gifts are has helped me gain insight into my motivation as I serve Christ and to understand my place in the church. It is important for the minister's wife to understand her special areas of gifting and to see how she is uniquely fitted for the role to which she is called.

The works of Oswald Chambers also greatly influenced me. Adrian and I read from Oswald Chambers' daily devotional book, *My Utmost for His Highest*,[4] for many years. Also, my mother gave me her collection of books by Oswald Chambers.

God has led me to pick up one of these books on many occasions when I needed help. Chambers had penetrating insights.

Family Background

You may have a wonderful, godly family background, or you may have some things you wish were different. I am grateful that I was raised in a

---

[4] Oswald Chambers, *My Utmost for His Highest* (Michigan: Discovery House Publishers, 1992).

home where my mother and father took me to Sunday school and church, but I still have things in my family background that I wish were different.

There was a split in my family's religious background, and there's a part of me that wishes that had never happened. I'm the only Baptist in my family, but God works all things together for good to those who love Him (Romans 8:28) because I married Adrian Rogers, who became a Baptist preacher.

I've learned to be grateful for the many wonderful factors in my family background. My family had a reputation for integrity, and my mom and dad were married to each other for sixty years before they died.

How about you? You can gain understanding by examining the differences in your family background—good or bad. God can use each of these factors in your ministry.

Training or Education

What are your areas of training or education? Have you taken music or art lessons? Did you attend or graduate from college? Have you taken courses in writing or speech? Have you had training in counseling, nursing, or teaching?

I went college for three years, and although I did not get my degree, I am a perpetual student. I love to study and read. I majored in Bible in college, and I love to study and teach the Bible.

I discovered areas of interest after I was out of school. I've read many books on Christian psychology and also marriage and the family, helping me counsel many women in the churches where we served.

I developed an interest in nutrition and have studied on my own in this area for over thirty-five years. This has improved the quality of my own life and helped me to encourage others.

I had always loved to sing but had no formal training. After I turned forty years old, I took voice lessons that helped me be a greater blessing to others as I shared the songs God had laid on my heart.

I encourage you to consider areas where you have a great interest. It's never too late to develop skills that can enhance your quality of life.

Appearance

I can't change my height, the color of my eyes, my facial features, the size of my feet, etc., but I can apply makeup properly, maintain a healthy weight, and wear stylish and modest clothes. Part of this I received from conception and can't change, but part of it is up to me, and I can improve it.

Life Experiences

Some of my life's experiences have been good. I was a pastor's wife for fifty-four years and was at five wonderful churches. I have traveled all over the world although I didn't think I would ever go anywhere. I have met four presidents of the United States. When Adrian was president of the Southern Baptist Convention, we were invited to a state dinner in the Rose Garden of the White House.

In life, bad experiences come with the good. Our two-and-a-half-month-old son, Philip, died. Divorce has touched at the very heart of our lives. Four of my best friends have died. God can use every experience in our lives; just wait and see. I want to encourage you to write down your life's experiences and wait and see who God will bring into your life to identify with because of what you have gone through. Some of life's experiences are painful and private and should only be shared privately when God gives the go ahead. Others can be shared publicly and be a great blessing to many.

Commitment Service

Now that you've taken a look at who you are in Christ, I encourage you to have your own private commitment service.

Romans 12:1–2 says, *"I beseech you therefore, brethren, by the mercies of God, that you present your bodies a living sacrifice, holy, acceptable to God, which is your reasonable service. And do not be conformed to this world, but be transformed by the renewing of your mind, that you may prove what is that good and acceptable and perfect will of God."*

Will you say before God: "I gratefully accept myself as God uniquely made me. Thank You, Lord. I yield myself to the Holy Spirit to be filled with Him." In other words, Romans 12:1 says, "*. . . that you present your bodies a living sacrifice.*" We'll call that:

Presentation

"I'm bringing 'who I am,' the person You have created me to be and to become. I'm making this presentation, this present, this gift of myself to You." As my husband has said: "I come not in sinful exaggeration, not in false humiliation, but in sober estimation!"

Transformation

Romans 12:2 says, "*. . . and do not be conformed to this world but be transformed by the renewing of your mind, . . .*"

PRESENTATION + TRANSFORMATION

Transform. This is where we get our word metamorphosis, which means where the inner nature comes to the surface. The inner nature of the caterpillar is a butterfly. When Jesus was transfigured, the same word is used and is translated "transformed" in Romans 12:2. He went through a metamorphosis. His inner nature was glory. That glory came to the surface.

What is the inner nature of a Christian? Jesus! When we're transformed, Jesus is going to shine through.

Romans 12:2 tells us, "*. . . that you may prove what is that good and acceptable and perfect will of God.*"

PRESENTATION + TRANSFORMATION = REALIZATION

Not self-realization
But Christ-realization

Oswald Chambers said, "I must be broken from my self-realization, and immediately that point is reached, the reality of the supernatural identification takes place at once, and the witness of the Spirit of God is unmistakable—'I have been crucified with Christ.'"[5]

Will you also tell the Lord: "I trust you to live Your life in and through me. I will continue to develop Your gifts to me."

[5] Oswald Chambers, *My Utmost for His Highest* (Michigan: Discovery House Publishers, 1992), p. 229. Copyright 1935 by Dodd, Mead & Co. Inc. Copyright renewed 1963 by Oswald Chambers Publications Association Ltd. All rights reserved.

CHAPTER 4

How to Have the Best Marriage in the World

I've been in love with Adrian Rogers for over sixty years. We were married for fifty-four of those years. I still have the love notes he dropped by my desk in the sixth grade.

I don't know on what day, week, month, or year it turned into the real thing, but it did! In high school, I often sang to Adrian. Two of our love songs were "Promise Me We'll Still Be Sweethearts after Graduation Day" and "You'll Always Be the One I Love."

How did I know? How can anyone know he or she will stay in love for a lifetime? We have a choice—a choice to say I WILL.

We will be composing our love song in the key of C. You will notice that each major point begins with "C."

I WILL BE COMMITTED

We promised to be faithful to each other. Adrian and I stood before a church full of people and before God and made a vow—a marriage vow.

"I Joyce, take thee, Adrian, to be my wedded husband, to have and to hold from this day forward, for better or for worse, for richer or for poorer, in sickness and in health, to love and to cherish 'til death do us part; and thereto I plight thee my troth" (or and thereto I promise you my faithfulness). It wasn't just good intentions; I meant every word.

We made a solemn vow to each other and we made it before God. It was based on God's Word in Romans 7:2: *"For the woman who has a husband is bound by the law to her husband as long as he lives."*

We Promised to Be Faithful to God

One of the songs sung at our wedding was the hymn, "Oh, Jesus, I Have Promised."[6] I changed it slightly to go this way,

> Oh Jesus, we have promised
> To love until the end;
> Be Thou forever near us
> Our Master and our Friend.
> We shall not fear life's trials
> If Thou art by our side
> Nor wander from the pathway
> If Thou wilt be our Guide.

When my husband conducted a wedding ceremony, he always told the story found in Matthew 7:24–27. The story was about the foolish man who built his house upon the sand and the wise man who built his house upon the rock.

The Bible tells of how the rains and the floods came and beat upon both of those houses, and the house on the sand fell flat while the house on the rock stood firm! Of course, that Rock is JESUS! I'm so glad we chose to build our home upon Jesus Christ, the solid Rock.

We made a promise to God on our wedding night that together we would be faithful to Him. Both of us signed a certificate promising to read

---

[6] Original hymn written by John E. Bode, 1868.

God's Word and pray together every day. Then we began our life together by doing just that. I can't say we never failed, but doing this was our lifelong pattern. If we ever failed, we began again.

Even after fifty-four years of marriage, we took time to read God's Word and pray each morning at breakfast whenever possible, and at night we prayed together before we went to bed.

It was also our purpose never to go to bed angry. It's impossible to pray together and be angry. Yes, the foundation to our marriage was Jesus Christ. He's the One who helped us to stay in love for a lifetime. He's the One who will help you to stay in love for a lifetime.

Remember, it's your choice. Say, "Lord, I WILL! I WILL be committed for a lifetime."

"We Promise" cards:

We Promise to read God's Word and pray together daily when at all possible.

We Promise to share and pray for the needs of each other, our family, friends, and acquaintances to whom God has led us to minister.

_____   _____
        Husband   *Wife*

                                 _____
                                    Date

Of course, it takes two to make this kind of commitment. But it can start with you—a desire in your heart. You can begin to pray. Your husband should be the spiritual leader and initiate this, but he may not. Pray that God will give you wisdom in approaching this subject. Don't make him feel inferior to you spiritually.

Perhaps you could research some simple devotional books and suggest something. It's not enough to be committed to each other to have a successful marriage, but that's the foundation.

As you are "composing your love song in the key of C," will you also say:

I WILL BE CONTENTED

My Master

I will be contented with loving and being loved by God alone. Psalm 63:1–5 tells of David's longing for God's love:

O God, You art my God; early will I seek You: my soul thirsts for You, my flesh longs for You in a dry and thirsty land, where no water is; Because Your loving kindness is better than life, my lips shall praise You. Thus will I bless You while I live: I will lift up my hands in Your name. My soul shall be satisfied as with marrow and fatness; and my mouth shall praise You with joyful lips.

In the following poem, God is speaking of how we are to be satisfied with His love.

BE SATISFIED WITH ME

Everyone longs to give themselves completely to someone;
To have a deep soul relationship with another
To be loved thoroughly and exclusively.

But to a Christian, God says, "Until you are satisfied, fulfilled, and content with being loved by Me alone;
Discovering that only in Me is your satisfaction to be found, will you be capable of that perfect human relationship.

Until you are both satisfied exclusively with Me
and the life I've prepared for you,
You won't be able to experience the love that exemplifies
your relationship with Me;
And this is perfect love.

I want you to have this most wonderful love;
I want you to see in the flesh a picture of your relationship with Me.

And to enjoy materially and concretely the everlasting union of beauty, perfection, and love that I offer you Myself.

> Know that I love you utterly,
> For I am God
> Believe it, and be satisfied,
> —Anonymous

My Mate

I will be contented with loving and being loved by my own husband. Song of Solomon 6:3 says, *"I am my beloved's, and my beloved is mine."* Titus 2:4 tells wives *". . . to love their husbands."*

Don't be dreaming up the impossible man (the best visible qualities in other men), and then be comparing this impossible man to your husband; do be giving up unrealistic expectations to God.

Oswald Chambers speaks about the "the discipline of disillusionment" in his book, *The Place of Help*.[7]

> Most of the suffering in human life comes because we refuse to be disillusioned. For instance, if I love a human being, and do not love God (as I should), I demand of that man or woman an infinite satisfaction, which they cannot give.
>
> Think of the average married life after, say, five or ten years; too often, it sinks down into the most commonplace drudgery. The reason is that the husband and wife have not known God rightly. They have not entered through the discipline of disillusionment into satisfaction in God. Consequently, they have begun to endure one another instead of having one another for enjoyment in God.
>
> The human heart must have satisfaction, but there is only one Being Who can satisfy the last aching abyss of the human heart, and that is our Lord Jesus Christ.

---

[7] Oswald Chambers, *The Place of Help* (Michigan: Discovery House Publishers, 1989); p. 52.

Be learning acceptance. Be realistic. He's not going to correct all his peccadilloes. Maybe he'll improve on some, but he will never be perfect, and guess what? Neither will you. He may keep picking his teeth until the day he dies. He may leave the lights on, squeeze the toothpaste in the middle, or leave his clothes on the floor. He may be an ultra-picky perfectionist, or he may be one who never picks up after himself.

Before God, accept him and his peccadilloes. Have an acceptance service. Remember, "for better or worse." Make a list of all of his good qualities. Begin to thank God and him for these good qualities.

When something irritates you, remind the Lord that you accepted him the way he is, and use the irritations as an opportunity to pray for him. For example, if he leaves the lights on, pray that he will be a light to the world spiritually.

My Material Possessions: Is Contentment Dependent on Things?

I will be content with such things as I have.

Hebrews 13:5 says, *"Let your conduct be without covetousness; be content with such things as you have. For He Himself has said, 'I will never leave you nor forsake you.'"* 1 Timothy 6:5b–8 says that there are some who are *". . .destitute of the truth, who suppose that godliness is a means of gain. From such withdraw yourself. Now godliness with contentment is great gain. For we brought nothing into this world, and it is certain we can carry nothing out. And having food and clothing, with these we shall be content."*

When we were first married, we lived in a twenty-five-foot house trailer without a toilet or shower. We had an outdoor bathhouse. But amazing as it may seem, I thought it was wonderful, and I was contented. Today I live in a nice house, and I am contented! But I am no happier now than I was then.

More convenient? Yes!
More comforts? Yes!
Happier and more satisfied? No!

Adrian and Joyce in front of their house trailer

I love this modern-day parable entitled "Dream House" from *Meeting God in Quiet Places* by F. LaGard Smith.[8] Let me quote just a portion. It speaks for itself!

> For several years now I've been enchanted by a particular house in the village of Stanton. Perhaps I should say that I'm enchanted by the setting of the house, because I've never even been inside the house itself. But its overall ambience is glorious—my perfect "dream house!"
>
> . . . But my excitement was short-lived, because I soon realized just how much of a dream house it really was.
> . . . It might as well have been Windsor Castle that I wanted

---

[8] F. LaGard Smith, *Meeting God in Quiet Places* (Eugene, OR: Harvest House Publishers, 2001).

to buy! But still today, I pause at the gate, look wistfully, and only reluctantly head for home.

"Reluctantly head for home?" Did I really say *reluctantly* with reference to my little cottage in Buckland that I have come to love? . . .

How silly I am to drool over my "dream house" in Stanton when I already live in a "dream house" in Buckland. . . . Do I never tire of wanting more? Will I never be content with what I have?

You've got to settle it in your own heart if you will be contented to successfully stay in love for a lifetime—not just live together under the same roof.

What Kind of Woman Are You?

Are you a greedy-for-gain woman—never content, always prodding your husband for just a little more? One day he'll wonder if you really love him, if you're satisfied with him, and what he can provide. I knew someone like that, and after many years, he left. I don't say he was right to leave. He wasn't. But he did!

Or are you a completely contented woman—satisfied with your husband and what he can provide?

Are you blessed and grateful? God may bless you financially. I never dreamed we'd ever own a home of our own—and I'm so grateful for the home I now have.

We married young and had three children in the seven years Adrian was finishing his schooling. In those years, we couldn't afford new clothes. I remember Adrian telling me back then, "Honey, one day I'm going to buy you a brand-new wardrobe."

Fast forward about twenty years. I remembered that comment, and it dawned on me that in the ensuing years, he had indeed bought me a new wardrobe. But you know, every year he got credit for buying me a brand-new wardrobe because I knew he really meant it many years before.

If God blesses and you're able to keep your priorities in order and have a nicer house and other things, fine! Just remember to be content with what you have.

And remember this! God just may have blessed you with more so you can give it away to those in need or to help those in faraway places to hear the gospel. We got to the place where we had a giving budget because we loved to give.

Keep composing your love song in the key of C.

I WILL BE COMPLETED

There are two aspects of being complete—God's Role and God's Rule.

God's Role

It is clearly stated in Genesis 2:18 that the role of the wife is to be a helper. *"And the Lord God said, 'It is not good that the man should be alone; I will make him a helper comparable to him.'"*

It doesn't say his slave, but his helper. She should be someone to help him, encourage him, and make him complete. First Corinthians 11:7–12 says, *". . . but woman is the glory of the man. For man is not from woman, but woman from man. Nor was man created for the woman, but woman for the man. For this reason the woman ought to have a symbol of authority on her head, because of the angels. Nevertheless, neither is man independent of woman, nor woman independent of man, in the Lord. For as woman came from man, even so man also comes through woman; but all things are from God."*

In other words, the man can't say, "I don't need you." Neither can the woman say, "I don't need you." We were made to be one—to be complete. But I am to be his *completer* not his *competer.*

God's Rule

We must ask the question, "Who is in charge?" In every area of life, someone is in charge—the manager in the department store, the mayor of the city, the governor of the state, the president of the country.

In the relationship of husband and wife, God had an original plan. It is clearly stated in 1 Corinthians 11:3: *"But I want you to know that the head of every man is Christ, the head of woman is man, and the head of Christ is God."*

God, the Father
Christ
The Man
The Woman

The MEANING of Submission

Submission isn't a dirty word. It simply means "equal worth" but not "sameness of function." This is one equal placing himself or herself under another equal to accomplish a task.

Galatians 3:28 states, *"There is neither Jew nor Greek, there is neither slave nor free, there is neither male nor female, for you are all one in Christ Jesus."*

The man and woman are of equal worth. There is no inferiority of the woman in God's sight. But this does not state that the male-female roles are abolished in Christ. Nowhere is the egalitarian philosophy—sameness of function—stated.

The PURPOSE of Submission

Submission is God's wonderful plan to maintain order in this world. In fact, everywhere you go, someone is in charge. If not, there would be chaos. And submission is God's role for the woman in the home.

The greatest example of submission was modeled by Jesus Christ. Philippians 2:5–8 says, *"Let this mind be in you which was also in Christ Jesus, who, being in the form of God, did not consider it robbery to be equal with God, but made Himself of no reputation, taking the form of a bondservant, and coming in the likeness of men. And being found in appearance as a man, He humbled Himself, and became obedient to the point of death, even the death of the cross."*

He was and is equal with God, the Father—equal in worth. He is God! But at the same time, in function, He submitted Himself to His Father. He became obedient unto death.

The RESULT of Submission

Philippians 2:9–11 tells us that *"every knee shall bow and every tongue confess that Jesus Christ is Lord, to the glory of God the Father."*

Matthew 5:5 says, *"Blessed are the meek (the submissive), for they shall inherit the earth."*

The INFLUENCE of Submission

To be a submissive wife doesn't mean that the wife should be a doormat, never giving her opinion. The Bible says that she is to be a helper. She has a point of view that her husband needs. She can be a mighty influence to make him be a success.

As she brings her input to the table, she needs to do it in a respectful fashion—never putting him down. She should motivate her husband, helping him to make wise decisions through her encouragement and sometimes her insights.

She should not manipulate him, using various subtle and deceptive means to get her way. In the book of Ecclesiastes, King Solomon was doing some research. He was looking for someone who sought after wisdom. He had probably looked high and low for the right woman who would inspire him to fulfill his potential. He observed hundreds of them with no success. He said, *"And I find more bitter than death the woman whose heart is snares and nets, whose hands are fetters. He who pleases God shall escape from her, but the sinner shall be trapped by her"* (Ecclesiastes 7:26).

He pictured a woman full of deceit and trickery. She sought ways to insure her selfish desires. When she caught her prey, she slipped her hands around his waist and neck. They became as chains. Her trickery deceived him, but he was nevertheless bound.

Many times, women resorted to deception since they didn't possess the physical strength of a man. Some women, even today, will use any evil means to accomplish their selfish projects. Jezebel was such a woman. She sank about as low as a woman can sink.

She misused the office of queen to possess Naboth's vineyard. She wrote letters in her husband Ahab's name and sealed them with the royal

51

seal. She even gave a spiritual command to proclaim a fast. She arranged for two false witnesses to testify against Ahab resulting in his murder. God's judgment was not immediate, but it was sure. She was a woman whose heart was "snares and nets."

Motivation versus Manipulation

God has endowed the woman with the unique role of motivator. Her husband is called on to be the main decision maker. She can inspire him to greatness. She can motivate him more than any other person through her love and admiration.

There is a fine line between motivation and manipulation. Others may not always be able to discern the difference. The outward acts may be the same—admiring him and doing thoughtful acts. But the woman who is a manipulator is doing these things to get her way. She thinks her way is always best.

The Holy Spirit inwardly motivates the Christian woman to do good works. He provides the inner spark that can be fanned into a flame. How wonderful that God uses a wife as an instrument of his motivational power.

If a woman is not controlled by the Holy Spirit, she will probably resort to manipulation. She may subconsciously try to imitate the supernatural force of the Holy Spirit. However, no woman can duplicate this force. How foolish she is to try. The end of manipulation is empty and unfulfilling.

Invite Christ to control your life, and you can become God's inspiring motivator. God will begin changing you into that "perfectly suited" partner to your husband and an inspiration to your children as you ask Him to cleanse your motives and put His will and His glory uppermost in your life.

The Submissive versus the Dominant Wife

In her insightful book, *Finding the Hero in Your Husband*, Dr. Julianna Slattery[9] draws the difference between a truly submissive wife and a dominant wife. She says that,

> . . . a submissive wife does not abandon her influence in her marriage. In essence a woman empowers her husband when she uses her influence and strength to help him to become a stronger, more confident and godly person.
>
> The dominant wife's motives may not be evil, but she cannot trust her husband's leadership. However, the more she dominates him, the less capable leader he becomes. The goal of the submissive wife is to convince him that he can trust her with everything he is.

I encourage you to read this book. It has many excellent insights and observations.

The ABUSE of Submission

You probably are asking this question, "Aren't there abuses? What about battered wives?" Yes, there are abuses. God didn't say the man should be a dictator, a tyrant, or an abuser. No, God said he was to be a leader, a protector, a lover.

Ephesians 5:25 says, *"Husbands, love your wives, just as Christ also loved the church and gave Himself for her."*

---

[9] Dr. Julianna Slattery, *Finding the Hero in Your Husband* (Florida: Faith Communications, 2004), p. 50.

The Solution to Abuse

We should not abolish the biblical principle of submission, but we should try to correct the abuse. The problem is sin! Abuses come to women because of sin.

Man is sinful—Unless he's saved and lives a Spirit-filled life, he becomes dictatorial, harsh, and selfish. Some have even gone to extremes in abusing and enslaving women.

There are extreme situations. I don't believe a woman should remain in an abusive situation. Others are "Mr. Milktoast" and refuse to take the leadership responsibilities.

Sinful man either refuses to give the woman her rightful, God-given place of "helper," or heaps too much on her.

Before you say, "Amen," you might have to say, "Oh, me!" Woman is also sinful. Unless she is saved and Spirit-filled, she can lead a manipulative, nagging, bossy, selfish life.

Sinful woman either refuses to give the man his rightful place of leadership or does too little in fulfilling her God-given role of helper.

There are two parts to the solution: giving up our selfish rights and allowing Jesus to be in control.

If Jesus is sitting on the throne of my life, and if Jesus is sitting on the throne of Adrian Rogers' life, the Rogers' kingdom will be at peace—not war.

Ephesians 5:18 says, *"be filled with the Spirit . . ."*

Ephesians 4:32 states, *"And be kind one to another, tenderhearted, forgiving one another, even as God in Christ forgave you."*

Remember—It's your CHOICE!

I WILL BE CONCERNED

I love to do many things. I love to speak and teach; I love to sing and write. I love to take video pictures and edit them. I would say that I'm pretty good in these areas. I can't say that I'm the best. In fact, I don't have time to be the best in all of these areas, and I may not have the innate ability to be the best. There *is* one area of my life where I aspired to be the *best*. I wanted to have the *best* marriage in the world. Do you?

One godly lady I know has had three husbands. Her first two husbands died. Now she has a comparison. But I don't have a comparison. I was married to the same man for over fifty-four years, and he was my one and only sweetheart. But I know that I had the best marriage in the world. In fact, I was married to the best kisser in the world. I've only kissed one man romantically, so how do I know? I just do!

Do you want the best marriage in the world? Then let me share with you some of "Joyce's Secrets to a Successful Marriage."

Joyce's Secrets

You have to want to be the best! It has to be a priority in your life. I told you that I didn't have time to be the best of everything, so I had to choose my priorities. I chose many years ago to have the best marriage in the world.

When I was in high school, I dreamed of the day when I would be married—when I would be Mrs. Adrian Rogers.

Back then, girls had hope chests. My grandfather gave me a beautifully carved chest that he had inherited. He knew I was in love and wanted to be married. I collected items and put them in that chest—crocheted doilies, pillow cases, and sheets my mama had made for me.

I remember collecting coupons off Mama's Pillsbury flour. When I had enough of them, I would send off for some knives, forks, or spoons, and then I put them in my hope chest.

You see, I longed for the day when I would be married to Adrian Rogers—Reverend Adrian Rogers. I was so thrilled that God had called him to be a preacher.

To Be the Best You Have to Study and Learn How to Do it Well

High school graduation

I studied on the subject of marriage for a long time. There are basically three study guides that I discovered are the best resources to help you have the best marriage:

1. The Bible

This is God's instruction manual for marriage. I've read the Scripture passages about marriage over and over again. Below are some of the main biblical principles for marriage. It would be a good idea to read these passages together during the next three months and take time to discuss them.

Genesis 3:20–21—The "leave and cleave" principle
Psalm 127—The "fruit of the womb" principle
Proverbs 31:10–31—The "virtuous wife" principle
Song of Solomon 2:5—The "romance" principle
Song of Solomon 4:12–16—The "pleasant fruits" principle
Song of Solomon 5:10–16—The "my beloved" principle
Romans 7:2—The "'til death do us part" principle
1 Corinthians 7:4–5—The "defraud not" principle
1 Corinthians 7:32–34—The "please your mate" principle
Ephesians 5:22–33—The "submission" principle
Ephesians 5:33—The "admiration" principle
1 Peter 3:3–5—The "inner beauty" principle

2. Christian books

Here are a few wonderful Christian books about marriage. Make sure the ideas you glean from these books agree, first of all, with the Bible, and then also with your personality.

To Have and to Hold by Jill Renich
Let Me Be a Woman by Elisabeth Elliot
The Five Love Languages by Gary Chapman and Ross Campbell, M. D.
Intimate Issues by Linda Dillow and Lorraine Pintus
How to Be Happy Though Married by Tim LaHaye
Building Your Mate's Self-Esteem by Dennis and Barbara Rainey
Love for a Lifetime by Dr. James Dobson
The Marriage Builder by Larry Crabb
Intended for Pleasure by Dr. Ed and Gaye Wheat
Finding the Hero in Your Husband by Dr. Juliana Slattery

3. The book of human nature

This book contains a careful and close-up study of your own husband—his likes and dislikes, his temperament and spiritual gifts, his idiosyncrasies, his strengths, and weaknesses.

This is a very important book. You should be "reading" it all the time because it is what enables each of us to have the best marriage in the world. You see, each one of our marriages is unique—so it can be the best in its category.

Pray for insight, wisdom, creativity, and strength to put into practice the foundational principles you learn from God's Word, ideas you gain from reading Christian books, and the lessons you have learned from your own book of human nature.

Biblical Principles

All the biblical principles I listed on the previous page are important, but in the following pages I will comment on only a few. Previously I listed the biblical principles in the order in which they are mentioned in the Bible. Here I will list them in order of importance, according to what I have read and observed.

The Admiration Principle

Ephesians 5:33 states *". . . let the wife see that she respects her husband."* I know personally that this is so. I remember an example that happened back when we were in junior high school. Adrian lived just two blocks from my house. I "just happened" to be looking out the window one day, and who do think was riding by my house on his bicycle—backwards? You guessed right. It was Adrian.

Many years later, after we were married, this incidence came to mind. I reminded him of it and asked him, "Were you riding backwards to impress me—just hoping I would look out and see you?" He replied, "Of course! I wanted you to admire me."

He also has told me he wanted me to think his sermons were good—that it meant so much to him when I bragged on them, no matter what anyone else said.

Oh, I have read about this, and I have heard about it. But I've experienced it. Ladies, it is true. A man's deepest need is to be admired by the one he loves the most.

Never, no never, criticize your husband in public. Do not do it in front of his friends, the church members, your children, or other family members. I knew of a minister's wife who criticized her husband publicly. He was very gifted, and so was she. I don't know why she thought this was appropriate. After many years, he had had enough of her criticism, and he finally divorced her. She asked his forgiveness and said she would change, but it was too late. I'm not saying he was right. He wasn't! He left the ministry. A home was divided, and lives were devastated. God was grieved and so was I.

We can know and believe these biblical principles, but if we don't know our own husbands, then we can't practice them effectively. So I want you to stop right now and take a few minutes to think about and write down qualities and abilities of your husband. They can be character or physical qualities, talents, and abilities—physical, emotional, or spiritual.

Do not list any of his weaknesses—only his strengths. Write down big things, small things, and medium-sized things. Then when you see him, day in and day out, tell him how much you appreciate one of these qualities or abilities. Don't mention that I encouraged you to do this—just do it! Tell him verbally, write a note, or give him a card. Do something creative.

> If he's good looking, tell him.
> If he's losing his hair, don't tell him.
> If he's creative musically or artistically, appreciate these abilities.
> If he's patient and kind, admire this.
> If he's a good leader, brag on him.
> If he prays effectively, tell him what a blessing he is.
> If he's a good father, appreciate that.
> Be grateful for his courage, his faithfulness, his generosity,
> for being a good lover, or for whatever your husband is and
> provides.

One Mother's Day, I wrote all of my children love notes. I included my husband. This is what I wrote:

> To Adrian
> To you, who first dropped love notes by my desk
> Who walked me home from school
> Who first held my hand
> And promised to love 'til death do us part.

> First it was one baby
> Then two and three
> Then four and five;
> You've loved me and you've loved each child.
> You were my lover, my husband,
> Then a father to our brood.

Adrian: Your name means "creative one."
I pray that God will continue
To use your life
To create love, unity, and faith.
Thank you for letting me be a mother!

Make a scrapbook to display his accomplishments. Tell his family (in front of him and behind his back) of things you appreciate about him or honors he has received that they may not know about.

Help your children to honor him. When my children were younger, they gave their daddy a trophy. At the bottom, these words were written: Best Daddy in the World. My husband received many honors in his lifetime. But I've heard him tell that his favorite award was for the "Best Daddy in the World." I wonder whose idea that was?

When Adrian was president of the Southern Baptist Convention, I wrote a simple little song for everyone to sing called, "We're So Proud of Our Pastor." Long after that occasion I would sing to him, "I'm so proud, I'm so proud, I'm so proud of my husband! I'm so proud, I'm so proud of God's man!"

Think of ways to encourage and appreciate your husband. When Adrian had a heart attack, I made a handwritten book of Scripture verses that he really loved. I have made many scrapbooks that showed his accomplishments. It wasn't hard to do because, indeed, I was so very proud of "my man of courage and conviction."

Say thank you frequently, for the small things as well as the big things. In prayer, praise and thanksgiving are inseparable. Even so, admiration and gratitude go hand in hand. They are different, but they are inseparable.

Your man needs to be respected and admired. You need to respect and admire him. The Bible tells us to do it, so let's get busy!

The "Pleasant Fruits" Principle

I'm also told that the second greatest need of a man is for sexual satisfaction. It might even tie for first place. And just because he is a minister doesn't mean he is not human. There are a lot of people who can meet some of his needs. But there is only one person whom God designed to meet this need—his wife.

As an older woman, let me give you a few practical tips I have learned through the years. Pay attention to:

1. How you look and smell. (See Song of Solomon 4:1–11.)

A man is more turned on by sight; a woman, by touch. So, ladies, keep yourself attractive. So many women let themselves go. They go around the house looking like an unmade bed. They gain too much weight. They don't fix their hair and face until their husbands have gone to their jobs. That is where they will see other women dressed their best.

It is worth it to get up fifteen minutes earlier so he can remember how nice you looked when he left home. Ladies, even in my seventies, I still tried to dress in pretty nightgowns and underwear. I wanted to look nice for him. He was my sweetheart, and he was special.

2. How you act. (See 1 Peter 3:3–6.)

We as wives should have *". . . a gentle and quiet spirit,"* so act like a lady—respectful and gentle. Watch the way you sit. Don't be a nag, throw tantrums, or be boisterous.

3. What you say. (See Song of Solomon 5:10–16.)

Read the Song of Solomon to each other at least once a year. It can be a refresher course in romance and intimacy.

Never stop telling him you love him. Tell him he's the best kisser in the world.

Express your gratitude and admiration. Admire his muscles (if he still has them), and tell him how strong he is.

Be sure you communicate and work through your differences. Don't say anything you will later regret.

4. What you do.

Years ago, I bought Adrian a poster with two lovey-dovey bears with these words at the bottom: "Love can turn a dreary day into a warm and cheery day." It stayed around for a long time, and then it finally got put away. I think it was when we moved to a new house. I found it the other day. It brought back such sweet memories.

Fix his favorite meal or dessert. Light a candle in the bedroom, and play soft, romantic music.

My husband's advice to wives was: Play "huggie bear and smacky mouth" often. Give him plenty of lovin' and hot biscuits.

Do little things that he likes. Before he comes home, look in the mirror, freshen up, and look nice for him. He is special! Always greet him at the door with hugs and kisses. We always kept this as a romantic ritual, even when we were in our latter years.

It is a good idea to read Christian books on sexual intimacy. Yes, the book of The Song of Solomon is a good starter. It would be an excellent refresher course for you and your husband to read out loud together once a year.

A book I would recommend is *Intimate Issues* by Linda Dillow and Lorraine Pintus. Every idea may not be in your comfort zone. I just skipped over those things I didn't think applied to me. But there are many good observations on the subject of sex in this book. I especially liked the question posed in the opening chapter: "What does God think about sex?"

Six answers from God's Word were given. God's voice declares:

I gave the gift of sex that you might create life.

"Be fruitful and multiply; fill the earth and subdue it" (Genesis 1:28).

I gave the gift of sex for intimate oneness.

". . . a man shall leave his father and his mother and be joined to his wife, and they shall become one flesh" (Genesis 2:24).

I gave the gift of sex for knowledge.

"Now Adam knew (had sexual intercourse with) Eve his wife" (Genesis 4:1).

HOW TO HAVE THE BEST MARRIAGE IN THE WORLD

I gave the gift of sex for pleasure.

"I am my beloved's and my beloved is mine . . ." (Song of Solomon 6:3).

I gave the gift of sex as a defense against temptation.

"The wife does not have authority over her own body, but the husband does. And likewise the husband does not have authority over his own body, but the wife does. Do not deprive one another except with consent for a time, that you may give yourselves to fasting and prayer, and come together again so that Satan does not tempt you because of your lack of self-control" (1 Corinthians 7:4–5).

I gave the gift of sex for comfort.

"Then David comforted Bathsheba his wife, and went in to her and lay with her . . ." (2 Samuel 12:24).

In the book, *Intimate Issues,*[10] the question is raised, "How can I relate when he's a microwave and I'm a crockpot?"

The answer is given, "Ask God to strike you with a severe case of the *'willies.'*"

I WILL deny my selfishness and respond to my husband.
I WILL give my body as a gift.
I WILL enjoy sex and praise God for creating this beautiful way to relate to my husband.
I WILL minister to my husband and think of his needs rather than my own.

Praise and thanksgiving are inseparable, so admiration and gratitude for your husband go hand in hand. They are different, but they are inseparable. You say thank you for the things he does for you and for the things he provides. You admire or praise him for his accomplishments and his character—for who he is.

---

[10] Linda Dillow and Lorraine Pintus, *Intimate Issues: Twenty-One Questions Christian Women Ask About Sex* (Colorado: WaterBrook Press, 2009), reprint edition.

To a man, his accomplishments express who he is. Be grateful for:

- The leadership he provides, spiritual and otherwise
- The security and stability he gives
- The physical things he provides day by day
- Special gifts—small or large
- Compliments he gives
- His creativity
- His courage
- His faithfulness
- For being a good lover or
- Whatever your husband is and provides

First Corinthians 6:19–20 says that our body is the temple of the Holy Spirit. We should therefore glorify God in our body and in our spirit, which are God's. Of course, your husband is a grown man and is directly responsible for taking care of himself physically—his exercise and eating habits, refraining from bad habits, but is there anything that you, as his wife, can do to help him?

You can encourage him in a gentle way. I encouraged Adrian to walk with me. It helped both him and me. It became a time where we talked about the issues that were relevant to both of us. It was a time when we held hands and fellowshipped together.

Also, he wanted to put some exercise equipment in our game room, so I encouraged him to do that. There is a fine art to discern between encouragement and nagging. Ask God to show you the difference.

Although you can't make him eat right, you can study about good nutrition, change your own eating habits, and provide healthy alternatives.

From time to time, I read nutritional tips and information to him. I have studied about natural foods, how to count calories, how to read labels, how to bake my own whole wheat bread, how to juice fresh fruits and vegetables, and which foods are rich in specific vitamins, minerals, etc. I'm constantly trying new, interesting, and delicious but nutritious foods. I've been into eating natural foods for over thirty years. I've been made fun of from time to time and ignored by some. But over the years, I've received more appreciation than ridicule, especially by my husband.

The Spiritual Oneness Principle

Last, but not least, is the importance of praying with your husband and praying for your husband.

First Peter 3:7 says, *". . . being heirs together of the grace of life, that your prayers may not be hindered."*

I told you that on our wedding night we signed a commitment card. We promised to pray together and read God's Word together every day.

In times of joy and times of sorrow
In easy times and difficult times
In times in the valley and times on the mountaintop

In times when we felt like it and times when we didn't feel like it. Yes, sometimes we failed, but we always began again. It is so important to pray with our husbands.

To pray for each other
To pray for our children, our grandchildren and yes, our great-grandchildren.
For mutual needs and friends
For missionaries and the lost around the world

After we were older and our children were out of the nest, we developed this plan for our prayer time together. Each day, we prayed for our children, family, and friends. Then we prayed "around the world"; we prayed for a different part of the world.

Sunday—North America, especially the United States
Monday—Central America
Tuesday—South America
Wednesday—Africa
Thursday—Europe
Friday—The Middle East
Saturday—The Far East

Our son, David, and his family were missionaries in Spain for eighteen years. We had a special prayer burden for Spain. We also knew other missionaries in different parts of the world, so we prayed for them by name.

Through the years, we traveled to a number of countries on mission trips. We met many national Christians and developed a deep spiritual bond. Of course, we prayed for them.

We also had a special prayer burden for Israel. We have Jewish and Arab friends. Some are Christians; some are not. We had a spiritual love affair with this Holy Land. We took about twenty-five trips there. There is a command to "pray for the peace of Jerusalem." We endeavored to do that. I still do!

It was one of my greatest joys and one of my greatest ministries to pray for my husband. Sometimes my prayers were unorganized; sometimes they were thought out. Sometimes they were ever so simple, like, "Oh, God, please help him; give him wisdom, protect him, comfort him, and guide him to know and do your will."

I remember some years ago riding in an air ambulance, going from Cozumel, Mexico, to Miami, Florida, after my husband had had a heart attack. I fervently prayed that God would heal him. How I praised God for answered prayer at that time. Take that man whom God has given to you. Magnify and admire his good points; minimize and pray about his weaknesses. Also pray about his strengths. Oswald Chambers said, "An unguarded strength is a double weakness."

In the Bible, there are examples of godly men who fell at the point of their strength:

David, at the point of his integrity;
Abraham, at the point of his faith;
Peter, at the point of his courage.

Pray for your man. He desperately needs your prayers.

Conclusion

These "secrets" are so simple. But if you don't practice them, they won't do you any good. It will take time, effort, creativity, love, forgiveness, and sacrifice. But it is worth it! It will indeed help to make your marriage the best in its category.

CHAPTER 5

The Value of Children

My husband and I had children before we had "things" because we placed a high value on them. After all, doesn't God's Word say, *"Behold, children are a heritage from the LORD, the fruit of the womb is a reward"*? (Psalm 127:3).

I'm so grateful for a husband who loved children. I remember his saying one time, "There's always room for one more." We wanted at least four children. We had five and several miscarriages. God took one of them, little Philip, to live with Him in heaven when he was just a baby. So I now have on this earth two boys and two girls. They are married and have nine children. At present, those children have six children with one baby, little Poppy Joy, in heaven. There are still prospects for lots more. Indeed, it is exciting!

My husband used to say that he wanted to take his children to heaven, that material things weren't going to make it. Well, he is waiting there for us, along with our little Philip and our little great-grandbaby, Poppy Joy Luce, who only lived for three hours.

The Sacrifice of Having Children

I'm not saying that it won't cost to have children. There's a lot of sacrifice involved. There's a sacrifice of time—time to do what we wanted, time for just the two of us, time to sleep in on days off. There's a sacrifice of things. We married when we were young, when we were both in college. Then there was seminary for my husband. That amounted to seven years that we were married while in school. In those years, we had three children and three miscarriages.

I didn't realize at the time that we were poor. Gradually, the clothes Daddy bought me to wear at college wore out or went out of style. But I've never regretted having children before I had things. I can't imagine life without Steve, Gayle, David, Janice, and even little Philip, who didn't live with us very long.

Many years have come and gone since having babies. Some of those days were hard. David and Janice are only sixteen months apart and were in diapers at the same time. When they were babies, we washed diapers and hung them on the line to dry and then folded them!

I can still remember one day when there was a mountain of unfolded diapers on my bed. A great miracle happened. Both of my babies went to sleep for their naps at the same time. I see it even now in my mind's eye. I took my hand and swept them onto the floor, dived into the bed, and took a nap myself.

Yes, life was very busy in those days. I also had an eight-year-old and a six-year-old. Adrian had to go to church early on Sundays, so I was left to get everyone ready by myself. I still remember that wonderful lady, Ann Monroe, who for a long time came by on Sunday mornings and took the three oldest children to church with her so I could get the baby ready by myself.

As I reflect on fifty-nine years of being a mother, thirty-two years of being a grandmother, and seven years of being a great-grandmother, I would give a resounding hoorah for motherhood! It is the greatest career of all. Truly, I am blessed. Grandmothering and great-grandmothering is a wonderful bonus!

Adrian loved being Daddy and PaPa. He didn't get to know the "greats," but he would have loved each one. He was there to greet little Poppy Joy when she took her flight to heaven. He loved his own children, and he loved the children at church. When he met them in the hallway at church, he would always stoop down to talk to them. The children loved to hear him preach. He had a special gift of speaking to the children and educating them at the same time. It was fitting that he was buried in a place that had a statue of Jesus holding little children in His lap.

Anything worthwhile requires a lot of skill, a lot of time, and a lot of sacrifice. And so it is with having and raising children. It's not all fun and games, but indeed, there is a lot of fun and games. Adrian loved to play and joke with the kids. He loved to play Monopoly, "apple tree," swing the little kids back and forth, and play "tick tock" like an old clock.

A Sense of Humor

One of the necessary ingredients in raising children is a sense of humor. My husband had a great sense of humor, and he helped develop mine. Our home rang with laughter. He loved to make up and tell stories. That wasn't my gift, but I loved to listen to him weave a creative tale.

We used to have a little sailboat when we lived in Florida. We kept it pulled up on the shore at our neighbor's house. It was big enough to either hold the two of us or to hold him and our two youngest children. One of David's best memories is when the three of them would go out in the sailboat and take turns adding to a story that their daddy had started. This is one way he taught the children to be creative writers and speakers.

He loved to tell jokes. I think he was programmed to remember them and to tell them at just the right time. He helped create a balance between having a good time and being a good person.

Teaching the Word of God

Yes, PaPa was a preacher, and his great passion was preaching the gospel—the good news about Jesus. He wanted all of his children and grandchildren to love Jesus and His written Word, the Bible.

While they were growing up, we tried many methods of family worship and teaching our children the Word of God. Adrian and the kids were very competitive, so challenging games like Bible baseball helped them learn Bible facts. We gave rewards for memorizing Scripture and learning the books of the Bible.

I remember when David's Sunday school teacher challenged his class to memorize the books of the Bible. He learned them backwards because he had already memorized them at home.

Teaching Through Music

I've always loved to sing. When our oldest son, Steve, was not quite two years old, we bought him a little record player. (There were no cassette or CD players back then.) The nearest Christian bookstore was fifteen miles away, and Christian records for children were scarce, and so were funds. But I remember buying a record player and then a record that had about twenty choruses about Jesus and the Bible.

By the time he was twenty-eight months old, he had listened to those songs over and over and we sang them together again and again. He had memorized them all. They were songs like "Jesus Loves Me," "Jesus Loves the Little Children," and "The B-I-B-L-E." He had another record he loved entitled, "Horace the Horse on the Merry-Go-Round." No wonder he grew up to love music and become a musician/composer.

The church is not a substitute for teaching your own children God's Word, but it can be a real encouragement. I remember that our minister of music, Jim Whitmire, challenged the children in his children's choir to memorize hymns. The one who memorized the most hymns won a brand-new hymnal. My daughter, Gayle, took on that challenge and won the hymnal.

My husband wasn't a musician, but he taught Steve his first song on the black keys of the piano when he was just five years old. The words went this way:

I went behind the turkey house
And fell upon my knees
I almost laughed myself to death
To hear those turkeys sneeze.

Then he taught Steve how to play the chorus to the hymn, "In the Sweet By and By" on the black keys. One day soon after that, we came into the room and discovered him picking out other simple hymns by ear. That's when we discovered he had an "ear gift." We started him in piano lessons soon after that with our church pianist. When he was just five years old, he composed his first song, "The Frog at the Show."

Scripture Memory

My youngest daughter, Janice, has a passion for memorizing Scripture. She works best on a challenge, so sometimes she and her friends or siblings competed in learning Scripture. She far surpasses me in this endeavor, although I'm sure it began when she was small and we encouraged her to learn Scripture.

She has memorized whole books of the Bible, dramatic Bible stories like David and Goliath, and well-known chapters like Hebrews 11 and Psalm 107.

One day a friend, Jesse McClerkin, was sharing that for years he had offered $1,000 to anyone who could memorize Psalm 119—you know, the longest chapter in the Bible, with 176 verses. It's all about the Word of God and obviously very difficult to memorize because he had never had a taker.

Well, when my daughter, Janice, heard this, she took his challenge. And when Janice told her married daughter, Rachel, who is also a whiz at Scripture memory, what she was doing, Rachel began to memorize the passage, too. In fact, Rachel passed up her mother and won the contest! I was there when Rachel quoted all 176 verses to our friend, Jesse, and he gave her the $1,000. Janice also finished learning this Psalm, and now they both have it hidden in their hearts.

A Special Gift

Janice also has a special love and gift for teaching Scripture to her children. She puts Scripture to familiar tunes and dramatic gestures to help them remember the wonderful promises in God's Word.

When going through a very difficult time in her life, Janice taught her two daughters, Angie and Rachel (ages three and seven at the time), Psalm 107 (forty-three verses). It's a difficult passage with very "adult" meaning. But they both learned it through creative means to help them through hard times.

Janice also taught them Hebrews 11. Her method was so effective that when Angie was in her first year of teaching Bible to eighth graders, she used the same songs and motions to teach her students this well-known and loved "faith" chapter. Mothers of even the eighth-grade boys told Angie they heard them singing it in their rooms at home. Can you imagine eighth-grade girls and boys singing this chapter in front of everyone at school? These truths have been taught and will be remembered for a lifetime.

Angie and Rachel are full-time moms now. By age two, their children were quoting Scriptures and singing songs about Jesus.

Scripture memorized as a child will one day "race to the rescue" when that child is broken hearted. I well remember that Mother's Day afternoon when little Philip was snatched into the arms of Jesus through sudden crib death. Immediately, God's Word came to mind. The first verse that came to me was Job 1:21: *"The LORD gave, and the LORD has taken away; blessed be the name of the LORD."* Then the twenty-third Psalm rushed to my heart and mind—verses I had learned when I was but a child. I discovered for the first time the deep and vital meaning of Psalm 23:4: *"Yea, though I walk through the valley of the shadow of death, I will fear no evil; for You are with me; Your rod and Your staff, they comfort me."*

It is so very important to teach our children to memorize Scripture when they are young and yes, even all of their lives.

Teaching Integrity

At the very core of our character is integrity. No matter how gifted you may be or how high your IQ is, if someone says, "But you can't believe a word he or she says," then your basic character is impugned. God's Word says, *"A good name is to be chosen rather than great riches, and loving favor rather than silver and gold"* (Proverbs 22:1).

How do we teach our children integrity, which amounts to a life of truthfulness? First, it is taught by example. My daddy was a quiet man. He didn't talk much. I'm not quite sure how he taught me integrity, but he did. It must have been by example day in and day out.

It was verified later in life by these two illustrations. My daddy, Guston Gentry, built a business for over thirty-five years. When he sold that business, the new owners kept his name: Gentry Bros. Paint and Glass Co. His name was prized, for he had built a reputation for integrity.

Recently, I attended my sixtieth high-school reunion. A former classmate wrote me that he had been in a civic club with my daddy many years ago. He wanted to tell me that although my daddy was a quiet man, he was known for his integrity.

When my parents died at the ages of eighty-five and eighty-six years, they didn't leave a large monetary inheritance. But more valuable than much earthly treasure was the legacy of integrity they left me.

Adrian and I wanted to pass down this legacy to our children. How did we do this? First, we did this by example—day by day. Some childish mistakes were overlooked, but one offense that always brought corporal punishment was lying. Second, God's Word was the back-up tool. It wasn't, "Be truthful because we say so" but "because God's Word says so!"

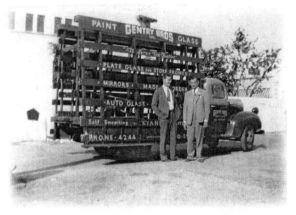

Gentry Brothers (Joyce's dad is on the right)

Here are some of those biblical principles:

- Proverbs 12:17—*"He who speaks truth declares righteousness, but a false witness, deceit."*
- Proverbs 12:19—*"The truthful lip shall be established forever, but a lying tongue is but for a moment."*
- Proverbs 13:5—*"A righteous man hates lying, but a wicked man is loathsome and comes to shame."*
- Psalm 51:6—*"Behold, You desire truth in the inward parts, and in the hidden part You will make me to know wisdom."*

The life of Joseph was a wonderful portrait of Jesus. Joseph wasn't a perfect man, but there was no major sin attributed to him. His life helps us to teach our children about how to live a life of purity; how to overcome unfair circumstances (Joseph was thrown into prison because a woman lied about him); how to be faithful in the most difficult of circumstances; how to forgive others who have wronged them; and how to recognize the sovereignty of God written over what was meant for evil.

The life of Samson teaches the consequences of bad choices and living an immoral lifestyle, of getting revenge for wrongs done instead of learning to forgive.

These examples and many others can be stored in the hearts and minds of our children. Then when life deals them an unexpected blow, these biblical examples and principles will be embedded deep within to enable them to stand in the storms of life, which will surely come.

I know! I've been there personally. My children, and now my grandchildren, have met Satan's onslaughts. I have seen them in the midst of horrendous storms in their lives. They have stood strong because their lives were founded on the rock of God's Word. I trust that as a mother and grandmother, I have had a vital part in this process.

Don't be deceived; life is hard! It is made up of the good and the bad. We must teach our children God's Word so they can successfully face the vicissitudes of life, whether small or great. They need to see Romans 8:28 mirrored in our lives. I believe this promise with all of my heart, and I want them to believe it too— *"that all things work together for good to those who love God, to those who are called according to His purpose."*

Discipline with Balance

Giving the appropriate amount and type of discipline is a fine art of balance. One needs a lot of wisdom to know whether the offense deserves a time-out in one's bedroom, a privilege taken away, or a spanking. Sometimes afterthought gives insight. It would be best to have an understanding ahead of time as to the types of offenses and what the form of discipline will be.

I do know that our children knew there were three offenses that would not be tolerated at all: lying, disrespect for one's parents, deliberate disobedience. The discipline for these offenses was a spanking. My husband required respect for me as the children's mother. They knew this, and I don't remember this rule ever being tested. They didn't want to discover the consequences.

It takes "the wisdom of Solomon" to determine the appropriate discipline for some offenses.

Avoiding the Consequences of Disobedience

I well remember when our sixteen-year-old son Steve wanted to go to a neighboring city to attend a concert featuring a famous guitarist. There were sure to be drugs among the attendees. Our son came home stating he wanted to hear this guitarist. His daddy wasn't home yet. I can still remember the tug of war I sensed in my son's spirit, and then he decided to not go without permission. At just that moment, his daddy drove up. I quickly told him the details and he immediately said, "Come on, son, I'll go with you." So they went together.

I believe that God gave my husband great wisdom on the spur of the moment. I'm so grateful that my son decided against disobedience, consequently avoiding the sure consequences.

"Son, Don't Put the Window Down"

There was an occasion when our family was in the car, and our son David let the window down in the back seat. Adrian told him to put it back up. After a while, the window went down again, and I was alarmed. I thought he had deliberately disobeyed. I turned around and expressed with great alarm, "David!" I knew he was in big trouble. But my husband was playing a trick, and he was one who had let the back window down. We all had a big laugh! A good sense of humor goes a long way in parenting.

We wanted to do the right thing in bringing up our children. I must admit that in looking back, we realized we had been too demanding in our expectations for our children, especially our oldest. They were not allowed even to go to a Walt Disney movie or to "mixed" swimming (and we lived near the beach in Florida). To make it worse, our children were the only ones in the church not allowed to do these things. I'm sure we felt like our example as pastor and wife was important.

When longer hair came along back in the sixties, we wouldn't allow our oldest son to even let his hair touch his ears. Consequently, there was some reaction to these overly strict requirements.

After graduation from high school, Steve went to Bible school in Capernwray, England. We happened to be traveling to the Holy Land via London, England, right after Christmas. We had purchased for Steve's Christmas present a Eurail Pass to travel through Europe to Germany for his Christmas break. He was going to spend the holidays with a friend who was from Germany.

We had arranged to meet him and visit for three days when going through London. When we arrived at the hotel where we had arranged to meet him, we saw him sitting in the lobby reading his Bible with his hair grown down to his shoulders.

We immediately agreed to not say a word. Why would we ruin our precious days with our son? We were learning to be more tolerant. We eventually laid down our expectations about his hair and our preferences for how he looked. I can't say this was easy, but looking back, it has become inconsequential. I can see that so much of it was pride—wondering what other people would think.

Over the years, Steve has changed his hairstyle many times. One time after we had moved to Memphis, he appeared for a special celebration at our church with an afro. I wondered how he could do this. Looking back now, it is humorous.

He has arrived with different styles of beards and different hairstyles. Nothing surprises me anymore. A good relationship is so much more important than these picky issues. I wish I had learned this sooner.

Years ago when he was in college, I called to tell him I was sorry for being overly strict in some areas. His daddy and I thought we were doing what God wanted us to do at the time. But now, I realize that it was what *we* thought others expected us to do. Much prayer and wisdom is needed to know the difference.

CHAPTER 6

Setting Proper Priorities

The secret to leading a truly fulfilling life is simply stated. It is setting proper priorities. How can this be done? Imagine with me a large glass jar. Picture also several big rocks, some gravel, sand, and water. You need to put these in the big jar. What should go in first? Of course, the big rocks should go in first, then the gravel, then the sand, and lastly the water.

Did you know that you may get your life filled with water, sand, and gravel, and have no room for the big rocks—the main priorities in your life?

You need to take time to determine what your priorities are. First, you should have some guidelines for determining your priorities. Let me suggest a number of factors:

1. The Word of God
2. Prayer and the leading of the Holy Spirit
3. The desires of your husband
4. The season of your life
5. Childcare (the number and ages of your children, if any)
6. Your health
7. Homemaking chores (grocery shopping, meal preparation, cleaning house, laundry, managing finances)
8. Church-related activities
9. Ill family members or dependent parent(s)
10. Job outside the home, if any

With these guidelines, then you should determine your priorities. Much prayer should go into this activity. The following is *my* list of priorities:

1. My relationship to the Lord
2. My husband
3. My children
4. Homemaking
5. Care of myself
6. Other family
7. Church activities
8. Friends
9. Hobbies
10. Other

It is one thing to determine your proper priorities. It is another to be able to work them out on a practical basis. Prayer and planning are the keys to making sure our lives are not lived haphazardly and consequently are unfulfilling. Here are some hints for planning:

1. **Write it down.** To be a good planner, you need to write it down, or you will probably forget something important.

    *   Keep a calendar. Decide what method is best for you—a pocket calendar, computer calendar, or an iPod. I personally keep my calendar on my computer.

    *   Then to help organize my day, I use a yellow legal pad. Of course, you can do this on your computer. I divide the page into three columns—calls, chores, errands.

    *   Invite the Holy Spirit to your planning meeting. Be sure and **pray over the things you need to do** for the day.

    *   Now, we're ready for the "big rocks." Of utmost importance is time alone with God at the beginning of every day. So my first "big rock" involves Bible study and

prayer. The next "big rock" is family time. At this point, you and your spouse should have regular "big rock" scheduling meetings.

- I believe that the wife/mother should research important family dates and be prepared to put these dates on the calendar. These dates will include ball games, recitals, graduations, school programs, vacations, date nights, family nights, etc.

In our early years of marriage, we did not have these regular "big rock" meetings, and it caused a lot of conflicts. In those days, my husband scheduled speaking engagements two to three years in advance. This also caused conflicts, so we adopted a family policy of his not taking engagements over a year in advance. Even then, sometimes, that caused a problem.

Something that I did not plan into my schedule was regular exercise and personal time for me. This brought stress into my life, especially since I had a number of young children close together.

2. **Don't get too busy!** This is easier said than done. My husband and I had different opinions about what was too much. We kept working on this area of our lives, and you will have to do the same.

Years ago, I counseled a young minister's wife who was on the verge of a nervous breakdown. She was going to college and trying to maintain a straight "A" average. She was working full time, plus she was a pastor's wife involved in church activities. Her husband was also attending Bible school full time.

I advised her to cut out some of the things she was doing. I lovingly asked her, "What are you trying to prove?" There were reasons for all these factors, and it wasn't that easily determined, but it was obvious that something had to go!

You and your husband need some diversion from the ministry. A date night every week and occasional overnight getaways should be priorities. Special occasions like birthdays, anniversaries, and Valentine's Day should be "big rocks."

Working It Out on a Daily Basis

It is necessary to first work out philosophies about priorities. But working these out on a daily basis is the real challenge. The "big rock" philosophy will eliminate many unnecessary conflicts. Make a list of things you need to do on a regular basis.

Establishing priorities and working them out on a daily basis requires a lot of prayer and living the Spirit-filled life, which involves confessing one's neglect and starting over again. Herein lies the secret of a fulfilling and successful life.

CHAPTER 7

Friendships in the Ministry

"Y ou shouldn't have best friends in the church." "The last pastor had a clique, and that caused a lot of trouble." These words took root in my soul, and for the next seventeen years in the ministry, I didn't have a best friend. Up until then, I had always had at least one best friend. In junior and senior high school, my best friends were Betty, Bertha, and Betty Lou. During my first year in college, Chrissy became my roommate and ultimately a precious friend.

Adrian and I got married our second year in college. We met Millie and Bob, and Millie became my best friend. She had a baby before I did, and when I was expecting, she taught me many things about becoming a mother.

After college, Adrian and Bob went to the same seminary, so we still saw each other from time to time. One night, Adrian was preaching in a nearby town. When he came home that night, I could tell something was seriously wrong. He had just heard that Millie had bulbar polio, which can be life threatening. We talked about it a long time before we went to sleep.

The next morning I was awakened by a phone call from Bob telling us that Millie had died. It was practically impossible to believe—my best friend had died. She was so young with two little girls, one and a half and three years old. I remember vividly my deep grief in losing my friend.

We continued our friendship with Bob and Barbara Barwick. Then in college and seminary we became best friends with Joe and Joyce Boatwright and Peter and Johnnie Lord. We all moved to Florida and lived close to one another for eight years.

We then moved to Tennessee, and I realized how much I loved these friends. We still saw each other from time to time and will always be lifetime friends, but I miss the fellowship we had on a regular basis.

When we left seminary and moved to a new church, I heard someone say, "The last pastor had a clique, and that caused a lot of trouble." Inwardly I declared, "I'll never cause trouble doing that."

So for the next seventeen years, I didn't have any best friends in my church. I had many friends with whom I ministered, but I never shared my deepest feelings with anyone. As I look back now, I realize that a number of ladies made efforts to be my friend, but I allowed them only limited access to my feelings.

I was in a very busy period of life, raising four very active children. I was involved with church activities, and Adrian was away from home a lot. He encouraged me to get a close friend, but I didn't really know how to do that.

I remember feeling frustrated, but at the time, I didn't realize that part of that feeling was the need for some good friends. God used a book by Oswald Chambers[11] to speak to my heart and give me insight into my problem. I was expecting my husband to be not only my husband, lover, and best friend—but my only friend. Oswald Chambers wrote, "The human heart must have satisfaction, but there is only one being who can fill the last aching abyss of the human heart, and that is our Lord Jesus Christ." God spoke to my heart that day saying, "You're trying to make Adrian play God in your life. He cannot meet every need that you have for fellowship."

It was still hard for me to make intimate friends. Finally, when we moved to another church, I determined that in this new situation I would make good friends. God did indeed send some wonderful friends into my life. Dot, Virginia, and I became very close. At first, Virginia and I met for lunch. I shared my vision for women's ministry and we dreamed together. Then she opened her heart and shared some of her deep heartaches with me. I gradually began to share my heart with her.

Dot has always been a great encourager, and I love her as if she were my own flesh and blood. Virginia and Dot were both ten years older than I,

---

[11] Oswald Chambers, *The Place of Help* (Michigan: Discovery House Publishers, 1989); p. 60.

but that never made a difference. Eventually, Dot moved away, but we stayed in touch. I call her my forever friend. She recently died, but I know that I will see her again.

When Virginia was stricken with cancer, I couldn't stand to see her suffer so much. With many tears and a broken heart, I asked God to take her home. When she died, I grieved the loss of another dear friend.

Then God sent Juanita into my life. Juanita was a wonderful musician, and she had a servant's spirit. At first, she was assigned to be my piano accompanist when I was asked to sing at a Valentine's Day party. When I started teaching the children's new members' class, she played the piano and helped in any way she could. She became one of my dearest friends. She loved my children, and I loved hers. We loved music, and we both loved the Holy Land. She enjoyed going with our group to this special land. She had the gift of hospitality and planned many lovely birthday parties in my honor and for others.

She read the book, *Sheltering Tree,* and nicknamed herself my sheltering tree, and indeed, she was such a refreshment to me. Juanita was a survivor, and when diagnosed with breast cancer, she gallantly fought it for ten years. As the end of her battle grew closer, she would come to class with portable oxygen to play the piano and write on the chalkboard for me. It was in those days I that I became her sheltering tree.

When Juanita went to be with the Lord, I planted a tree in our church courtyard with a simple brass marker at the foot that said, "Sheltering Tree." Before she died, I told her what I planned to do, and she was so pleased.

It is still difficult for me to initiate friendships, but God has been so good to send special friends to me. I believe that God means for us to have special friends with whom we can share our joys and sorrows and to help us bear our heavy loads. Even Jesus had His special friends—His disciples. He even had an inner circle—Peter, James, and John—and close friends whom He greatly loved, such as Mary, Martha, and Lazarus.

I encourage you to have friends who are intimates. Ask God to send you the right kind of friends. However, always have a smile and be friendly to everyone. Don't rush to greet your best friends when you are at church. This is intended not to discourage friendships, but to avoid jealousy by only fellowshipping and sitting with best friends.

I not only want to have special friends but I also want to be a good friend. The Scripture says, *"There is a friend who sticks closer than a brother"* (Proverbs 18:24), and indeed, *"Better is a neighbor nearby than a brother far away"* (Proverbs 27:10).

CHAPTER 8

The Imperative of Godly Mentoring

We hear a lot about the need for mentoring. Let's begin by asking some simple questions: What? Who? and How?

What Is Mentoring?

My definition for mentoring in general is "influencing someone else to a standard of excellence in a particular field." The dictionary says that a mentor is "a wise and trusted counselor."

But what is *godly* mentoring? I believe it is "influencing someone else in spiritual growth, to guide and influence someone to become like Jesus."

I guess we would assume that our mentors would be wise and trustworthy, but in these days, we cannot assume anything.

Who Should Be Our Spiritual Mentors?

Ideally, our parents, grandparents, and other family members should be our first spiritual mentors. But what if our parents or other family members aren't Christians?

We can choose godly friends. We can search for a godly, Bible-believing pastor of integrity and conviction. Then we can look to godly, dedicated Bible teachers.

Models of Mentoring

The apostle Paul said in 1 Corinthians 11:1, *"Imitate me, just as I also imitate Christ."* That could have sounded egotistical. But Paul was saying, "Only follow me if I am following Christ." You see, Christ is the one and only perfect mentor. We'll talk more about this later.

Philippians 3:17 says, *"Brethren, join in following my example, and note those who so walk, as you have us for a pattern."* The apostle Paul was a man who had been filled with hatred, pride, and had even committed murder. Are we to follow his example? But wait, he was changed—changed by the living Christ. We are to follow his example *after* Christ, not *before* Christ.

I never had the luxury of having a one-on-one mentor. The closest I ever got to having mentors was a couple who were my youth leaders— Julia and Ryland Mahathey. They met with me on a weekly basis for about a month to help me learn Scriptures, and then they timed me on how quickly I could find these passages.

As I began to think on this subject, I realized that I had been mentored by some of the greatest Christians. Some of them are dead, and some of them are still living. Some of them are well known, and some of them are unknown to most of the world. Some of them I knew personally, and some of them I did not know.

I decided to make a list of some the people who had most influenced me to become like Jesus and the greatest lesson they had taught me.

- My mother—to be a seeker after God
- My daddy—to be known for integrity
- My sister, Doris—even as a widow—how to trust and rejoice in Jesus' love every day
- My missionary son David and his wife, Kelly—how to be a "world Christian"
- Roy Hession, in his life-changing little book, *The Calvary Road*—how to die to self

- Jill Briscoe—how to step out in faith to do the impossible
- Elisabeth Elliot—how to live courageously and joyfully in the midst of great trial and heartache
- Elizabeth Tson—how to be willing to die for Jesus
- Kay Arthur—how to love and better study the Word of God
- Vonette Bright—how to reach out to other women and influence them for Christ
- Andrew Murray—how to live a life of absolute surrender
- Major Ian Thomas—how to live the Christ life

Finally, the people who taught me the most about becoming like Jesus:

Oswald Chambers—He was a man whom I never knew personally. He died in 1917 when he was only forty-three years old. He influenced me greatly through his books. His devotional book, *My Utmost for His Highest*, is the most popular devotional book of all time. I read out of it almost every day.

My mother gave me her collection of his books. It is my greatest inheritance. I have about forty-five of his books. God has used his writings to speak to some of my greatest heart needs.

One of the greatest lessons I learned from him was: "No one can understand us completely but God. If you try to demand that someone understand you completely, you are trying to make them play God in your life."

Biddie Chambers—the wife of Oswald Chambers. The lesson I learned from her was "how to greatly influence your world for Christ if you don't care who gets the credit." It was she who compiled *My Utmost for His Highest*, the all-time best-selling daily devotional book. David McCasland, the author of the latest biography of Oswald Chambers, said, "It should have been entitled, *Our Utmost for His Highest*."

She took down everything he taught in shorthand. After he died, it became her life's work to get his works published. Before she died in 1966, fifty books had been published that bore Oswald Chambers' name, but never hers. What a challenge this woman has been to my own life.

Last, but not least, is my husband, **Adrian Rogers**, who was my husband and pastor for fifty-four years. I cannot stop with just one lesson that I learned from him. There were many, but I am going to list five that greatly impacted my life:

1. How to treasure God's infallible Word and how to discover Jesus in all of its pages
2. How to be courageous and stand for truth at any cost
3. How to have a sense of humor
4. How to live with a positive attitude even in the midst of life's darkest circumstances
5. How to PACE myself spiritually

How Do We Become Effective Mentors?

How do we most influence those around us to be like Jesus? I believe the very best way is by example.

Does Character Count?

Does character count in those who lead and influence our lives? Of course it does! Is anyone perfect? No, no one but Jesus. But He has used other imperfect people, and He will use you even when you fail, if you truly repent.

-   He used David after he repented.
-   He used Peter after he repented.
-   He used Moses, Abraham, Jacob, and many others!

These people still suffered the consequences of their sin. Because He loves you and me, He will have to discipline us along the way, when we sin.

Character Qualities of a Godly Mentor

If we are going to lead by example, we must possess certain character qualities. Let me mention six that are absolutely imperative for a godly mentor:
1. WISDOM

Proverbs 4:7–9 says, *"Wisdom is the principal thing; therefore get wisdom.*

And in all your getting, get understanding. Exalt her, and she will promote you; she will bring you to honor, when you embrace her."

The Bible tells that wisdom is the main thing. There is worldly wisdom and godly wisdom. Godly wisdom is seeing from God's perspective. His wisdom helps us to see the beginning of sin. Most people don't get it until it's too late—when sin is so obvious and has worked its destruction.

I wrote a book in 1980 entitled, *The Wise Woman.* The subtitle was, "How to Be One Woman in a Thousand." The Bible tells us in Ecclesiastes 7:25, 27–28 that Solomon was looking for someone with wisdom. He could only find one man in a thousand. However, he could not find even one wise woman in a thousand.

This observation occurred to me—Solomon had seven hundred wives and three hundred concubines. That adds up to one thousand women. I think that he was looking in the wrong place, don't you?

I want to be one of the few—"one woman in a thousand"—who is wise. Do you? You can be! The pastor's wife holds a unique place of influence. She needs a lot of wisdom.

2. INTEGRITY

My husband wasn't perfect, but he was definitely a man of integrity. He grew into being a man of integrity. Jesus made him into such a man. I have known him since the sixth grade, but I didn't know his private faults and sins back then. He only showed me his good side.

It's only because he later told on himself that I know that when he was younger, "before Christ," he lied, cheated in school, and stole some things. But "after Christ," God convicted him of these things, and he repented and changed. I remember about twenty years after he became a pastor that God reminded him of a time when he stole a few pennies off his aunt's dresser. He wrote her, confessed, and returned the money. When we long for a life of integrity, these so-called small sins are important. Don't dig into your past trying to dredge up past sins. Just ask God to show you if there is something you should deal with. Don't worry; if there is, He will.

My husband loved pastors. At conventions, the delight of many young pastors was to speak to him. Many times, they would say, "Just give me a word."

It is difficult to lay a lot of wisdom on someone in a few seconds. After many years and many brief encounters with pastors, Adrian had honed his advice down to one word—integrity. He would say, "Make sure you have integrity." What God wants is a heart that loves to be pure—to be filled with truth.

Lying was first introduced in the Garden of Eden. It was in contrast to God's commands. Satan asked Eve this question: "Has God said that you should not eat of every tree of the Garden?" Satan began by trying to make Eve doubt God's Word. He twisted His Word. It was ever so subtle. God said that Adam and Eve could eat of all the trees of the garden—except one.

He also tried to make them feel deprived. They were surrounded by all kinds of beautiful and luscious fruit. They were not deprived at all. Only one tree was denied them. It was a test, and they failed the test.

Satan also spoke against God's motives. He said, "He knows that you will become like Him, knowing good and evil. He's withholding this from you." Satan is the great deceiver. They wouldn't become like God by disobeying God. God did want them to know the difference between good and evil, but His way—by choosing good. Then and only then would they truly know the difference.

The Half-Truth

Then there is the concept of the half-truth. Some would not call it an out-and-out lie—but an acceptable half-truth. But do you know what? I was always taught that a half-truth was a whole lie, weren't you?

Do you remember the story of Abraham, Sarah, and King Abimelech in Genesis 20? Abraham and Sarah journeyed into the land of Gerar, where Abimelech was king. Sarah was very beautiful and so to protect himself, he told a half-truth and said that Sarah was his sister. He got her to participate in this half-truth also.

This half-truth, which was really a whole lie, almost got him, Sarah, the king, and his entire kingdom into big trouble. Abimelech took Sarah and was going to marry her, but God appeared to him in a dream and said, "Don't touch that woman. She is another man's wife—Abraham's wife. If you don't give her back, I'm going to kill you and all of your people." So he gave her back in a hurry.

You see, it was a <u>half</u>-truth. Sarah was his father's daughter, but not the daughter of his mother. But he did not tell all of the truth—that she was indeed his wife.

Do you think that you can engage in telling half-truths? You had better watch out. This could destroy your life. Instead, I encourage you to pray along with the Psalmist in Psalm 16:1–3: *"Preserve me, O God, for in You I put my trust. O my soul, you have said to the LORD, 'You are my LORD, my goodness is nothing apart from You.' As for the saints who are on the earth, 'They are the excellent ones, in whom is all my delight.'"*

The best lie is the one nearest the truth, but mixed with serious error. All false cults are masters of this deception. The Jehovah's Witnesses say that Jesus is the son of God. But when pressed, they will tell you they do not believe that Jesus *is* God.

The followers of Islam say that Jesus was a good man but only a prophet. They even acknowledge that He was born of the Virgin Mary, but they deny that He died and rose again.

Christian Scientists declare that "sin is the figment of your mortal imagination" and that "the blood of Jesus was no more efficacious when he was hanging on a tree than when it was flowing through his veins." They have a glossary in the back of their book, *Science and Health with Key to the Scriptures* by Mary Baker Eddy. In it the meanings of many commonly accepted words have been changed, thereby deceiving many.

Two Mormon missionaries came to my door years ago. The first words they said to me were, "We believe the gospel just like you do." I knew what they believed, so I politely replied, "No, you don't." They told about "another" Jesus, not the one I know and that the Scriptures tell about.

Satan is the father of lies. Jesus is the Truth! By choosing Jesus, you will know Him who is the Truth. Then and only then will you be able to discern evil—but not by experiencing evil. In knowing Jesus, the Truth, is the way to know good because there is only One who is good, and that is God. Jesus is not only the Truth; He is God!

All false cults deny that Jesus is God, although they will acknowledge His good teachings. But Jesus Himself said, *"No one is good, but One, that is, God"* (Matthew 19:17).

The Belt of Truth

Ephesians 6 describes the armor of God. The first piece of armor that we are to put on by faith is the belt of truth. It is so very important. Many other things in our Christian life depend on TRUTH. It is foundational.

Jesus said in John 8:32, *"And you shall know the truth, and the truth shall make you free."* Yes, Jesus is the TRUTH, and He will set you free from enslavement to sin. Sin may give you a few thrills in the beginning, but then it enslaves you. Jesus is the only One who can break the shackles of sin and set you free.

I've known those who lied to their mates and were unfaithful, then they repented, got saved, and lived a brand-new life. How thankful I am for God's marvelous grace. But how much better it is to have lived that life of integrity and not to have been unfaithful.

Some will say that everyone tells half-truths. Some pastors lie about their church attendance. It's so common that some will refer to it as "ministerially speaking." There should never be such a thing.

Jacob was a deceitful man. His name literally means "deceiver." But he wanted to be a godly man. He wanted his father's spiritual blessing. There were bad results from his deceit, and God had to cripple him so he would lean on his Maker and become a man of integrity. God changed Jacob's name to Israel (Genesis 35:1), which means, "Prince of God." He was given twelve sons. Out of them God fashioned a nation of chosen people.

King David is known as "a man after God's own heart." He truly loved God and never worshipped idols. But he allowed deceit to creep into his life. Along with the sins of pride and lust, David fell into the sins of adultery and even murder. Then he tried to lie his way out of these horrible sins. God would not excuse him just because he was the king.

God forgave David because he truly repented. His repentance became as well known as his sin. It is written in the Bible for everyone down through the ages to read. His repentance is recorded in Psalm 51. Foundational in his repentance was truth. He prayed in verse 6, *"You desire truth in the inward parts, and in the hidden part You shall make me to know wisdom."*

Ten of Jacob's sons became great deceivers. They hated their brother, Joseph, for he was obviously his father's favorite. So these ten brothers plotted how they could deceive their father. Actually, most of them wanted to murder Joseph, but Reuben talked them out of it.

Instead, they threw him into a pit and sold him to a caravan of travelers going to Egypt. Then they tried to cover their sin. They killed a wild animal and put the blood on the precious "coat of many colors" that his father had given him. Then they told their father they had found Joseph's bloody coat and that a wild animal must have killed Joseph.

Yes, jealousy led to deceit and for years, they thought they had gotten by with their lie. They cared not one wit about their father's deep grief.

Their deceit caught up with them one day. There was a great famine in the land of Canaan. Their father sent them to Egypt where he had heard they had plenty.

Joseph was unlike his brothers. Even though he was unjustly treated, Potiphar's wife lied about him, and had him cast into prison. He maintained his integrity and purity. Through circumstances arranged by God, Joseph became mighty in power, next only to the Pharaoh.

Joseph's brothers were brought before him, but they didn't recognize their brother, who had become a ruler and deliverer in Egypt. But Joseph had pity on them and forgave his brothers, after testing them severely.

He realized that God uses even the bad circumstances of life to bring about His will if only he would maintain his integrity, which he did. He said to his brothers, who trembled before him, fearing for their lives, *"You meant evil against me; but God meant it for good"* (Genesis 50:20). The life of Joseph is looked upon by many as a "portrait of Christ." God honored Joseph greatly for being a man of integrity.

3. PURITY

When we normally think of purity, we automatically think of sexual purity. That is certainly part of it, but not the most important part.

Matthew 5:8 says, *"Blessed are the pure in heart, for they shall see God."* I used to think this verse pointed to heaven, when one day we would see God. That is certainly a part of this truth, but I believe that the fulfillment of this promise can begin now—for those who are pure in heart, single minded, they will be able to perceive God now.

Psalm 73:1 says *"Truly God is good to Israel, to such as are pure in heart."*

Proverbs 21:8 says, *"The way of a guilty man is perverse; but as for the pure, his work is right."*

Yes, purity of heart will work itself out in *sexual* purity. In Proverbs 7, Solomon tells how he looked through his lattice one day and saw a young man void of understanding. He went to the house of a harlot. He yielded to the words of her flattery.

Proverbs 7:25–27 gives this warning: *"Do not let your heart turn aside to her ways, do not stray in her paths; for she has cast down many wounded, and all who were slain by her were strong men. Her house is the way to hell, descending to the chambers of death."*

The sexually impure man or woman driven by sexual desire is also lacking in wisdom and integrity. You see, they are all linked together. Have you known some—even spiritual leaders—who were ensnared by sexual sin? I have. It can destroy your ministry and your influence.

Spiritual Lust

Did you know that there is also *spiritual* lust? It is unholy ambition—wanting things, even spiritual things, *my* way, *now*. These are closely linked together in leaders who are not filled with the Holy Spirit. As wives, we should be very careful lest we encourage this in our husbands.

Oswald Chambers spoke to this: "Remember lust can be spiritual. Lust disputes the throne of God in us—'I have set my mind to this or that, and I must have it at once.' Lust (the spirit of—I must have this thing at once) can have no part or lot in the house of God.

"Too many spend their time in educating themselves for their own convenience—'I want to educate myself, and realize myself.' No! I must use not use the temple of God for the convenience of self-love; my body must be preserved from trafficking for myself. One of the hardest scourges comes here.

"Goodness and purity should never be traits that draw attention to themselves but should simply be magnets that draw people to Jesus Christ."[12]

---

[12] Oswald Chambers, *My Utmost for His Highest* "March," (Michigan: Discovery House Publishers, 1992).

4. HUMILITY

Proverbs 30:13 says, *"There is a generation—Oh, how lofty are their eyes! And their eyelids are lifted up."* Pride was the sin that first caught Satan. He thought that he was too wise and too beautiful to be anything but in the place of God. Of the seven things in Proverbs 6:16–17 that God hated, pride was listed first.

Proverbs 29:23 says, *"A man's pride will bring him low, but the humble in spirit will retain honor."*

Proverbs 15:33b tells us, *"The fear of the Lord is the instruction of wisdom, and before honor is humility."*

The secret of humility is to pass all the honor on to Jesus when we are honored. We should stand in awe that God would ever use us, and give all the glory to Him. I remember many times when Adrian and I would drive up to the church, Adrian would remark, "I can't believe that God has let me pastor this church."

5. COURAGE

God said to Joshua after the death of Moses, *"Have I not commanded you? Be strong and of good courage; do not be not afraid, nor be dismayed, for the LORD your God is with you wherever you go"* (Joshua 1:9).

Did you know that there are some who have wisdom and can discern the truth but do not have the courage to stand for the truth? My husband said to some who were trying to manipulate things to win an election in the Southern Baptist Convention, "We don't have to win; we have to do what is right."

When asked to compromise to bring peace to the Southern Baptist Convention, he gave these memorable words: "We don't have to get together. The Southern Baptist Convention doesn't have to survive, I don't have to be the pastor of Bellevue, I don't have to live. But I'm not going to compromise the Word of God."

I was so proud to be married to this man of conviction and courage and to stand by his side and cheer him on.

6. FAITHFULNESS

First Corinthians 4:2 states, *"Moreover, it is required in stewards that one be found faithful."*

Oswald Chambers said, "We are determined to be successful; the apostle Paul says that we are called upon to be faithful."[13]

Our mentors must be known for keeping their word. We must be known for keeping *our* word. Will you keep your marriage vows? Will you abide by your contracts? Don't be careless about making promises, declarations, or covenants.

Some serious words are given in God's Word about making a vow (Numbers 30:2; Ecclesiastes 4:4–5) and then not keeping our word. Especially in the ministry, we should be very careful about this. Our word tells who we are at the very core of our being.

What if your mentor, teacher, spiritual leader, or even your pastor/ husband fails in this respect? What should you do then? Care enough to confront them in love. If they won't listen, you must keep on loving them and praying for them. Perhaps you will even have to go to others in authority for help.

What if you or your husband fails? Come to Jesus in confession and true repentance. D. L. Moody said, "When your repentance is as well known as your sin—God can begin to use you again." Don't try to step back in at the same level of influence you once had. Be tested and tried, and then let God, not you, promote you. You *can* be used in a lowly position.

Lamentations 3:23 tells us that God's faithfulness is great. We can always depend upon Him to keep His promises.

If we are becoming more like Him, we too will be faithful.

Wisdom, integrity, purity, humility, courage, and faithfulness. All of these character qualities equal a holy life—a life like the Lord Jesus Christ. Actually, He is the only perfect mentor!

First Peter 2:21–24 says, *"For to this you were called, because Christ also suffered for us, leaving us an example, that you should follow His steps: Who committed no sin, nor was deceit found in His mouth; who, when He was reviled, did not revile in return; when He suffered, He did not threaten, but committed Himself to Him who judges*

---

[13] Oswald Chambers, *The Servant as His Lord*, (Oswald Chambers Publications Association, 1972).

righteously; who Himself bore our sins in His own body on the tree, that we, having died to sins, might live for righteousness—by whose stripes you were healed."

Someone has said, "The Bible is a *Him* book. It's all about Him!" Open it and begin to read and to study about Him. Look for Jesus in the entire Bible.

Study the names of God. They will tell you what He is like. Personalize these in your own circumstances. It will revolutionize your life.

Study the gospels—Matthew, Mark, Luke, and John. Read them over and over again. Ask God to show you how wonderful He is. Yes, Jesus is our Magnificent Mentor to bring us to God. Remember, He is the way, the truth, and the life. No one comes to the Father except by Him (John 14:6).

The message of a song greatly influenced my life many years ago. It became my prayer.

OH, TO BE LIKE THEE[14]

O, to be like Thee, Blessed Redeemer
This is my constant longing and prayer;
Gladly I'll forfeit all of earth's pleasures
Jesus, Thy perfect likeness to bear.

O, to be like Thee! O, to be like Thee,
Blessed Redeemer, pure as Thou art;
Come in Thy sweetness, Come in Thy fullness
Stamp Thine own image deep on my heart.

Will you accept the challenge to be growing into the likeness of Jesus? Will you look to those mentors who will be godly examples and pointing others to Jesus?

---

[14] Hymn, "O to Be Like Thee" written by Thomas Chisholm (1897), music by William Kirkpatrick.

Joyce teaching new members' class

Will You Be a Mentor?

Is God leading you to a one-on-one relationship with someone to guide and influence for Christ? Is God leading you to teach and mentor children, young people, young married women—being an example to them and teaching them biblical principles to guide them in their walk of faith?

I taught a children's new members' class for over forty years. A couple of years ago I ran into Danielle, who was sixteen years old at the time. She was in my new members' class when she was seven years old. Every time I see her at church, she puts her arms around me and tells me how much she loves me. How rewarding it has been to realize that I have made an investment in the life of this young woman when she was but a child.

Will you begin today by offering a simple word of blessing or encouragement, a note, a letter, a phone call, singing a song—even over the telephone (I've done this lots of times), a book, or a Scripture?

Grammy and her girls (grandchildren and great-grandchildren)

It is imperative that we provide godly mentoring to this generation—to our generation of children and grandchildren and yes, great-grandchildren.

We must be qualified, not perfect, but blameless so that we can be a godly example! Will you begin today?

What Part Can a Wife Play?

You can't make your man live truthfully and be known as a man of integrity. But you can be an example and one who does not hinder him.

We can honor our pastor/husband by admiring him for this quality and telling him so. We can encourage him to stand for truth at all costs even if it means we will suffer inconveniences.

I was so proud to be married to a man of courage, conviction, and integrity. He stood for the truth of God's Word, but he also stood for truth at all levels.

God used him greatly. I believe that truth was the foundation on which his whole life was built. The foundation was the Man who was known as *the* truth—Jesus Christ, his Lord.

As pastor's wives, we can live our own lives of integrity. I remember a father who was known for his honesty in business. My mother was also known for her integrity. I don't remember on which day I chose to be a woman of integrity, but I know that I did. Each of us must choose for himself.

When I was in high school, I was influenced by this poem by Edgar Guest entitled, "Myself."

MYSELF

I have to live with myself, and so,
I want to be fit for myself to know;
I want to be able as days go by,
Always to look myself straight in the eye;
I don't want to stand with the setting sun
And hate myself for the things I've done.

I don't want to keep on a closet shelf
A lot of secrets about myself,
And fool myself as I come and go
Into thinking that nobody else will know
The kind of man I really am;
I don't want to dress myself up in sham.

I want to go out with my head erect,
I want to deserve all men's respect;
But here in this struggle for fame and pelf,
I want to be able to like myself.
I don't want to think as I come and go
That I'm bluster and bluff and empty show.

I never can hide myself from me,
I see what others may never see,
I know what others may never know.
I never can fool myself—and so,
Whatever happens, I want to be
Self-respecting and conscience free.

It should be taken for granted that a pastor and his wife are "truthful to the core." A lack of truthfulness will manifest itself in small and large ways. If we are not truthful in the small things, we won't be truthful in the big things.

Recognizing an error and calling it to the attention of the grocery clerk is just as important as your pastor/husband not exaggerating the Bible study attendance.

I love Psalm 101:2b: *"I will walk within my house with a perfect heart."* Also a favorite of mine is Psalm 145:18: *"The LORD is near to all who call upon Him, to all who call upon Him in truth."* I want God to be near me, don't you?

A pastor desperately needs the gifts of discernment and wisdom. Before God will bestow these much-needed gifts, he must be pure and honest. This kind of life must be lived daily, coming to Jesus for daily cleansing and filling with the Holy Spirit. The pastor's wife is an important part of this life of integrity. She needs to stand alongside him, being known as a woman of integrity and wisdom.

CHAPTER 9

Preparing for the Future

Adrian and I had arrived at the next stage of our lives—retirement. It was not easy for my husband to arrive at the appropriate time. He changed his mind several times. It created some emotional roller-coaster times for me. I just wanted him to make up his mind and stick to it.

I finally had to lay down this desire to know before the Lord and leave it there. Oswald Chambers' books have been used on numerous occasions to help speak to my deepest needs. I had read this particular book before, but it was never so relevant to my life's circumstances as at this difficult time. The name of the book was *Not Knowing Where*, which dealt with the life of Abraham. Certainly Abram's wife, Sarai, was married to a man who was a Bedouin and had to be ready to "pull up roots" at any time, for she and her husband were living in tents and moving whenever God spoke.

In the earlier years of ministry, we had moved after briefer times. But for the last thirty-two years, we had stayed in one church. I had taught the children's new members' class all of these years. I was now teaching the children of the children I had taught a number of years before. I liked being in a familiar setting. I didn't know exactly what I would do when we retired.

Adrian had many areas of service that he wanted to pursue after retirement. He wanted to continue his television and radio ministry, to preach in places where he may be invited, and especially to help train pastors. He and our oldest son, Steve, were planning to have Pastor Training Institutes with fifty to a hundred pastors at a time. Adrian wanted it to be "up close and personal." I was going to teach the wives, along with a few friends whom I had enlisted to help me.

We had already taught in four of these institutes. I was excited to be doing this, as well as he. Our son, Steve, had suggested that his daddy have the institute professionally filmed just a month after his daddy retired. What a miracle of grace this was.

We never dreamed that several months after Adrian retired, he would be diagnosed with cancer. He had hardly been sick a day in his life before a mild heart attack caused by a genetic heart arrhythmia several years before he retired. His father had survived two similar heart attacks and lived until age ninety-two. Adrian seemed to be fully recovered and was doing very well.

We cannot question these things. I'm just grateful that he did not have to linger and suffer. He was diagnosed with cancer in April and died seven months later on November 15, 2005.

Adrian thought he would spend at least ten more of his retirement years training pastors in these three-day institutes.

Steve and David in India with nationals

When his daddy died, Steve was left holding this videotaped institute, not really knowing what to do next. He then decided that at least God wanted him to edit the sessions. Then some doors of opportunity opened to show these videos (twenty-one hours of teaching that reflected fifty-four years of experience in the pastorate).

First, an opportunity came in Kenya, Africa, to train 350 pastors. Steve accompanied Chris Hodges, who had a meeting already scheduled there. The pastors didn't know who Adrian Rogers was. After the first day, they were calling him the "man of God" and asking for more of his teachings. Then he and his missionary brother, David (who had been in Spain for eighteen years as a church planter), took the institute to India, where it was overwhelmingly received. They trained about twelve hundred pastors there. Then Steve went with Chris to Nigeria and Ethiopia. Adrian's teachings were well received everywhere they were taken.

Consequently, the institute was translated and dubbed into Spanish. Circumstances brought my son, David, home. An opportunity arose to take the Spanish version to Venezuela, South America. Adrian's television and radio program, *Love Worth Finding* (in Spanish, *El Amor Que Vale*), had been dubbed and broadcast into Central and South America for twelve years; therefore, pastors all over those countries knew who he was.

David speaks fluent Spanish so he, along with a friend, David Ripley, took these materials first to the leaders in Venezuela and then to the leaders in UBLA (the Union of Baptists of Latin America) that met that year in Costa Rica. They were all thrilled with the opportunity to use Adrian's teachings to train pastors all over Central and South America. Steve, David, and David Ripley most recently took the DVDs and trained 625 pastors in Paraguay and then Uruguay. They each promised to train seven more pastors.

Today, many other doors are opening. Adrian would never have dreamed that his two sons would be taking the Pastor Training Institute all over the world. God gave Steve a 20/20 vision for the year 2020 to translate the institute into approximately twenty languages. Recently, the Nazarene denomination adopted these Pastor Training materials to train their church planters in Europe and Asia, translating the *Pastor Training Institute* into over twenty languages. What a miracle!

No, I don't understand why God took Adrian away when there were so many things in ministry to do. We can't question God. I'm excited for him that he's with his Savior, whom he dearly loved. Toward the end he said, "It's a win-win situation! Heads I win! Tails I win." He won!

His favorite gospel song was "Victory in Jesus." Probably ten thousand people sang it at the end of his celebration service. The theme I adopted for that service was "Come to Jesus." He had passionately pleaded for people to "Come to Jesus" during all of the years of his ministry. Now the call came to him: *"Come to Me, all you who labor and are heavy laden, and I will give you rest"* (Matthew 11:28). "Come to Jesus" were the words that I had placed under his name on his memorial marker.

When the disaster happened that trapped thirty-three miners in a mine in Chile, South America, in 2010, a man working on the rescue effort was also an evangelical Christian. He contacted his pastor to ask for spiritual help for these men. The pastor contacted the Spanish Christian radio station where my husband's messages, which had been translated into Spanish, were being broadcast. They sent some of my husband's messages down into the mine. Two of those men were saved as a result. Recently my daughter, Gayle, and her husband, Mike Foster, were in Argentina, working with the Word of Life missionary organization. They said that everyone they came in contact with knew of Adrian's radio and television ministry, *Love Worth Finding*. What a miracle!

How grateful I am that even from beyond the grave, Adrian is training pastors all over the world to call multitudes to "Come to Jesus."

I can't issue this plea exactly as he did. There was a passion with which he made the plea that made it unique. But I want to spend the rest of my life calling others to "Come to Jesus!" I challenge you to do the same.

CHAPTER 10

God's Not Finished with Me Yet!

It has been seven years since God took my pastor-husband home to live with Him. I still miss him greatly and think about him every day. But I'm not lonely, because I consciously—by faith—claimed my Maker to be my spiritual Husband. I feel His presence and experience His peace every day.

God has helped me every day and has given me hope for my tomorrows. He has shown me that He's not finished with me yet. As a wife, my life revolved around Adrian. Since he's gone, I'm discovering who I am now and what God wants me to do in the years I have left.

I taught the Bible for fifty-six years—first to teenagers, then adult women, and then to children for over forty years. I was a leader in women's ministry, helping to begin the movement of women's conferences in the Southern Baptist Convention. I also loved to sing in the choir.

I am now a member of an adult women's Bible class. I have passed my leadership baton on to the younger generation. From time to time, I am asked to speak to various women's groups—pastors' wives, widows, women's conferences, and seminars. I am helping to enlarge the widows' ministry in my church and am a part of my church's prayer ministry. I still sing in the choir and will do so as long as I am able. I love to sing His praises.

I am a mother, grandmother, and great-grandmother. I love taking part in the lives of my children, my grandchildren, and great-grandchildren.

I am a word person. I'm always writing down my thoughts, experiences, and insights from God's Word, hence, this book for ministers'

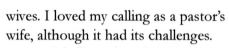

Hedgeville Women's Conference
Danville, Kentucky

wives. I loved my calling as a pastor's wife, although it had its challenges.

I believe that the answer to all of life's challenges is found in a daily, intimate relationship with God. I endeavor to meet with Him every day.

He wants me to reach out to others who are grieving and hurting and point them to the One who will bear their burdens. He wants me to sing my love songs to Him, my Maker and spiritual Husband and Lover. He wants me to praise Him and to be grateful for all the blessings He has brought my way.

He wants me to rejoice in the blessings of my family, my friends, and my church. Oh what joy they have brought to my life as they have surrounded

Joyce and her dog, Akie

me with their love. And yes, for my little dog, Akie, who loves to greet me at the door when I get home.

Isaiah 54:5 tells me that *"the God of the whole earth"* is my spiritual Husband. Indeed, He is my Protector, my Provider, and my Peace. Best of all, I can experience His Presence and claim His Promises. I could not be more blessed. "Thank You, Lord!"

CHAPTER 11

Lessons I Learned from Adrian

For fifty-four years, Adrian was both my husband and my pastor. I learned many things from him. He dug many nuggets from the Word of God that I highly treasure. He taught me how to do the same.

I listened to him explain the Word of God week by week. I figure that for fifty-four years, at fifty-two weeks a year, three times a week that it amounted to 81,324 times that I heard him preach.

As I was preparing a message on mentoring, I thought about lessons that I learned from him. I made a folder and put it on my computer desktop. Whenever I would think of another lesson, I would add it to my list. So far, I have written fourteen lessons that I learned from Adrian. Some of these lessons were by observation and example and came about as I listened to him preach week in and week out. Here is the list:

1. How to treasure God's infallible Word and how to discover Jesus in all of its pages
2. How to discern truth and make wise decisions
3. How to be courageous and stand for truth at any cost
4. How to live life to its fullest and to believe that no obstacle is too great for God
5. How to have a sense of humor, not take myself too seriously, and be able to laugh and enjoy life
6. How to live with a positive attitude of faith, without complaining, even in life's darkest circumstances

111

7. How to have a standard of excellence and think creatively (to think outside the box)
8. How to handle sacred things with respect
9. How to think logically and organize my thoughts
10. How to see the importance of pleading for people to "Come to Jesus"
11. How to dream "impossible" dreams and with God's help involve others to bring them to pass
12. How to be interested in people, from the smallest child to the oldest. He would make this simple statement that always drew other people in and made them feel important: "Tell me about you!"
13. How to be spontaneous and to lay down my planned agenda every now and then
14. How to PACE myself spiritually

Let me comment on a few of these lessons.

How to Treasure God's Infallible Word and How to Discover Jesus in All of Its Pages

Now, I'm sure that our home church believed in the infallibility of the Scriptures. It just wasn't an issue.

However, we were not taught how to discern and identify liberalism. So we both went off to our state Baptist university totally unprepared for the neo-orthodoxy being taught. And I might add that fundamentalism was greatly derided. But Adrian sat with his Bible in hand and began to notice that some things they were teaching did not agree with the Scriptures. So, he began to ask questions. I might add here that he was born with an inquisitive, logical mind. He began to take a stand for the Word of God and ended up being a champion for the inerrancy of the Scriptures in the "Battle for the Bible" in the Southern Baptist Convention.

We both majored in religion at our Baptist university, and I'm grateful for many wonderful things that I learned about the Bible. Here are a few things we did *not* learn:

- The infallibility of the Scriptures
- The types of Christ in the Old Testament and how to discover Jesus in all of the Bible
- The Spirit-filled life
- The pre-millennial return of Christ
- The Old Testament names for God and how they related to our personal lives
- A devotional love for Jesus

I don't know when Adrian first began to learn about the types of Christ, but I think his favorite type of Christ in the Old Testament was Joseph. It was my favorite too. I loved his sermon, "The Gospel According to Joseph."

He taught me to love the hidden truths in God's Word—how Jesus was portrayed. Adrian would often say, "Standing somewhere in the shadows you'll find Jesus."

He loved the name of Jesus. He would say, "I love the way it just fits on my tongue." He was a Jesus man. He loved to preach about Jesus and discover Him in the Bible. It wasn't an original saying, but he loved to say that the Bible was a Him book—it was all about Him!

Largely because of Adrian, I am a Jesus woman. Oh, how I love that name. I love to hear and sing about His name. By Adrian's preaching and by his life, he taught me to love Jesus more.

Tragedy stuck our lives when we were very young. I was just twenty-five years old and he was twenty-six. He was newly graduated from seminary. We had been at our new church for just three weeks. It was Mothers' Day. The sudden crib death of our little baby, Philip, cast us on Jesus in a way we had never needed Him before. We hungered after Him. We longed to know Him better.

Out of this brokenness, we began to discover the secret of the Spirit-filled life, and Adrian began to preach these truths. We discovered these truths together. I can't separate Adrian from how I learned, and I'm so grateful that I believed all of God's Word was true, so that I could claim all of His promises.

Adrian not only grew to be a man of deep conviction, but also grew to be a man deeply devoted to Jesus.

How to Be Courageous and Stand for Truth at Any Cost

Adrian developed into a very convictional man. He had been courageous on the football field when he was in high school. Therefore, it was not a surprise that he was courageous in his stand for God's Word.

So I'm asking, will *you* be courageous and stand—stand for truth, stand for what is right even if it costs you your livelihood and your very life? Ladies, will you be courageous and stand by your man? Will you encourage him?

Perhaps you know of Joseph and Elizabeth Tson of Romania. They were exiled during communism. We met them in this country. After communism fell, they returned to Romania and our church took a group of about 180 people on a mission trip there. Adrian preached three citywide crusades there in 1991.

I'll never forget after dinner one night in a hotel in Romania Joseph told this story. During communism, he came home one evening after having been interrogated and warned by the authorities and said, "Elizabeth, you know what they can do!" And she replied, "Then go and die, Joseph, and I will die with you!"

That story deeply touched my very innermost being that evening. In private, I remember saying to the Lord, "Lord, if that ever happens in the United States, I know that Adrian will be on the hit list. Please, oh please, let me be like Elizabeth."

Well, Adrian has been spared, and I am still here. You are still here. Will you cry out with me, "Oh God, I want to be faithful even unto death!" Ladies, stand by your man!

Even though Adrian was a deeply convictional and courageous man, he had a tremendous sense of humor and was a lot of fun to live with.

How to Have a Sense of Humor, Not Take Myself Too Seriously, and Be Able to Laugh and Enjoy Life

Adrian had a great memory for some things—names, sermon outlines, illustrations, poetry, hymns, Scripture, and jokes! We had a running contest. He would say, "Joyce, name a subject and I'll tell you a joke." I never named a subject for which he couldn't tell a joke!

114

He liked to do silly things with me. Perhaps it created a balance to his more serious life. He was very creative, and he used that creativity to give our lives a lot of fun. I really miss his jokes, his stories, and his pranks!

I guess the funniest thing he ever did was when I got up in the middle of the night and had this brilliant idea. He put his head under the covers and his feet on the pillow, hoping that I would do just what I did—lean over and kiss his foot.

We must have sat up in bed and laughed for twenty minutes. Every time I think of that occasion, I still want to laugh.

He established *The Adventures of Teddy*. He gave me a number of bears, but the significant one was named Teddy. What else? One day after he came in from work, he called for me to come to the bedroom. Teddy was sitting in an upside down umbrella, hooked over the fan in the bedroom, which was turned on. It was so funny!

I wanted all of my children to see it, so I left Teddy up in the umbrella almost a month. One day, Izetta, who helped with my cleaning, said, "Teddy's sure having a long ride."

The "Love Bear"

Then there was the "love bear." One Valentine's Day, Adrian gave me a little bear that had these words on his front: This "bears" my love. He had the idea that we should take the "love bear" and takes turns hiding him. We tried to best the other person. Sometimes the love bear showed up in the cereal or the refrigerator.

The "love bear"

115

My "best" was one Father's Day. While everyone was singing and greeting one another, I had our worship leader, Jim Whitmire, hand the love bear to Adrian. No one but Adrian, Jim, and I knew about the love bear. But I was so satisfied that I had "bested" him.

You couldn't "best" him, however. He was too creative. While on a mission trip to Moscow, Russia, we were in the office of the mayor of Moscow. I was taking pictures when the vice-mayor walked across the room and handed me the love bear. I couldn't believe it. I couldn't help but laugh and laugh.

He loved to make up stories. Sometimes before we would go to sleep at night he would say, "Name a subject!" I'd name some silly subject—like a bird on a telephone wire. He would weave some creative story that could have been good enough for a storybook. After he died, I tried to remember these stories and couldn't. I concluded that they were stories told just for me.

Adrian was a romantic.

It all started in the sixth grade when he dropped love notes by my desk. I still have some of those notes.

On our forty-fifth wedding anniversary, he told me he wanted to take me on a special trip, just in case we didn't make it to our fiftieth. I loved Switzerland. We would sometimes add on several days in Switzerland to the Holy Land trip. So we decided that just the two of us would go.

We rode trains, wore blue jeans, dragged our own suitcases, and stayed in small hotels. I'll never forget those twelve whole days with Adrian, and we didn't see one person that we knew.

On that trip, he instigated the "casting of the flowers." We rode a little red cog railroad to the top of Mt. Rigi near Lucerne. The mountain was filled with wild flowers. He picked a bouquet of wild flowers for me and I for him. Then he started at the letter "A," and would name a character quality for me and then cast a flower over the mountain. Then I would do the same for him until we went through the entire alphabet.

We went back to this same place two more times and cast flowers. It was one of my most treasured memories. We took a grandchild with us one time, and she videotaped us casting flowers.

A written "tribute"

After Adrian died, I was thinking one day that I wish Adrian had written down something special for me. Then one day I decided to look through some of the old home videos. I discovered that Adrian had not only written down a tribute for me, but that he had read it to me on Christmas morning in front of the children and grandchildren. My daughter, Janice, had videotaped it. He would read for a while, and then he would cry and then hand it to me. I read for a little while and then would hand it back to him. Then he would read and cry and hand it back to me. Then we would hug.

Living in my "fog," I hadn't remembered. Then I remembered where that little book was—right on the shelf in my study.

Adrian and Joyce in Switzerland,
where they cast flowers

Oh, what a treasure!

Do you recall that classic rhyme?

Roses are red; Violets are blue.
Sugar is sweet, And so are you!

The last thing Adrian ever wrote for me was in the hospital. I had it framed. This is what it said:

Violets are red; Roses are blue.
I'm all mixed up, But I love you!

At the National Religious Broadcasters' meeting this past year, I noticed that I was sitting at the table next to Chuck and Cynthia Swindoll. I observed that they were holding hands under the table. I leaned over and tapped them on the shoulder and said, "Don't! Don't ever stop doing that!" If I am ever walking in back of a married couple holding hands, I will say the same thing.

Yes, we loved to hold hands when we were sweethearts in school and when we were "older" sweethearts. The way I see it, you never get too old to hold hands. It will always be one of my sweetest memories.

How to Live with a Positive Attitude of Faith, Without Complaining, Even in Life's Darkest Circumstances

Adrian was a very positive person. He didn't complain—not once during his illness. Not that it would have been wrong if he did. Adrian was always there for me. When I was weak, he was strong. He would say, "Not to worry, Joyce! Everything will be all right."

Toward the end, I stood at his bedside and said to him, "Not to worry. I'll be all right!" I don't know if he heard me or not, and I didn't know exactly what all of that entailed. But I knew in the innermost recesses of my being that God would be there for me. And He has been!

Adrian and I both loved the names of God. Of course, our favorite name was Jesus! I love to sing about Jesus. He loved to preach about Jesus and passionately plead for people to "Come to Jesus."

We also loved the Old Testament names for God. My very favorite Old Testament name for God is Jehovah Shammah, which means, "The LORD is there." Some years previously, a man in our church, Riad Saba, who was a jeweler fashioned some banner pendants with Old Testament names for God.

Adrian gave me one, *JEHOVAH SHAMMAH*, that I highly treasure. There is a Scripture engraved on the back of this pendant. It is one of my favorites. I'm sure it's one of yours—Isaiah 43:1–3. It says: *"Fear not: for I have redeemed you; I have called you by your name; you are Mine. When you pass through the waters, I will be with you; and through the rivers, they shall not overflow you. When you walk through the fire, you shall not be burned, nor shall the flame scorch you. For I am the* LORD *your God, the Holy One of Israel . . ."*

I am not a composer, but I am a lover of music and a lover of the Word of God. On several occasions, the Lord has given me a simple melody to go with a simple but profound message I have discovered from His Word. Some months ago, He spoke to me as I was studying this passage again. Here are the words:

I'LL BE THERE

When you pass through the waters, I'll be there.
The rivers shall not overflow you. I'll be there.
When you walk through the fire, you shall not be burned.
I'll be there! I'll be there!

For I am the LORD your God.
I have redeemed you,
Called you by your name.
I am JEHOVAH SHAMMAH!
You are mine, so I'll be there.

I'll be there, I'll be there
Fear not, for I am with you.
I'll be there!

And then my youngest daughter, Janice, and her family gave me the name, JEHOVAH SHAMMAH and its meaning to go over my bed. My granddaughter Rachel designed it for me. It daily reminds me of this wonderful truth—that God is there for me and has promised to never leave me nor forsake me.

Plaque over Joyce's bed

How to PACE Myself Spiritually

Adrian taught me how to PACE[15] myself spiritually. I pray this almost every day when I am getting out of bed to greet my Lord and greet the new day. It is in the form of an acrostic.

---

[15] Taken from *What Every Pastor Ought to Know Workbook* by Adrian and Steve Rogers and the Pastor Training Institute (2006), p. 84.

P raise (I praise You, Lord that You gave Yourself *for* me)

A ccept (I accept that You gave Yourself *to* me)

C ontrol (I'm under Your control)

E xpect (I'm expecting it to be a great day)

Then I will vary my prayer in each of these areas as the Lord directs me for that day. He not only taught me how to PACE myself, but he taught our church. He also taught this simple tool to all the pastors who came to his Pastor Training Institute.

In Conclusion

Adrian wanted to finish well. He wasn't a perfect man, but more than anything he longed to be like Jesus. He loved Jesus with all of his heart, and he loved to invite people to come to Him.

I want to spend the rest of my life pleading for others to come to Jesus and lay their sins, their sorrows, and their suffering at His feet.

I have been greatly inspired by Adrian's life to follow Jesus more closely and to love Him more dearly.

What are you learning from that man whom God has given to you? I'm sure that it's more than you ever dreamed.

I'd like to close with the poem that Adrian probably quoted more than any other during his ministry:

Adrian and Joyce's retirement--Adrian's kiss (one of Joyce's favorite pictures)

Adrian and Joyce's 50th wedding anniversary
(another one of Joyce's favorite pictures)

Friends all around me are trying to find

What the heart yearns for, by sin undermined;

I have the secret, I know 'tis found

Only true pleasures in Jesus abound.

Jesus is all this poor world needs today

Blindly they grope, for sin darkens their way;

Oh to draw back the grim curtains of night

One glimpse of Jesus and all will be light.[16]

---

[16] Harry Dixon Loes, *Hymns of Faith*, "All Things in Jesus" (Hope Publishing Co., 1980), p. 182.

CPSIA information can be obtained
at www.ICGtesting.com
Printed in the USA
LVOW08s0521300617

539652LV00001B/17/P